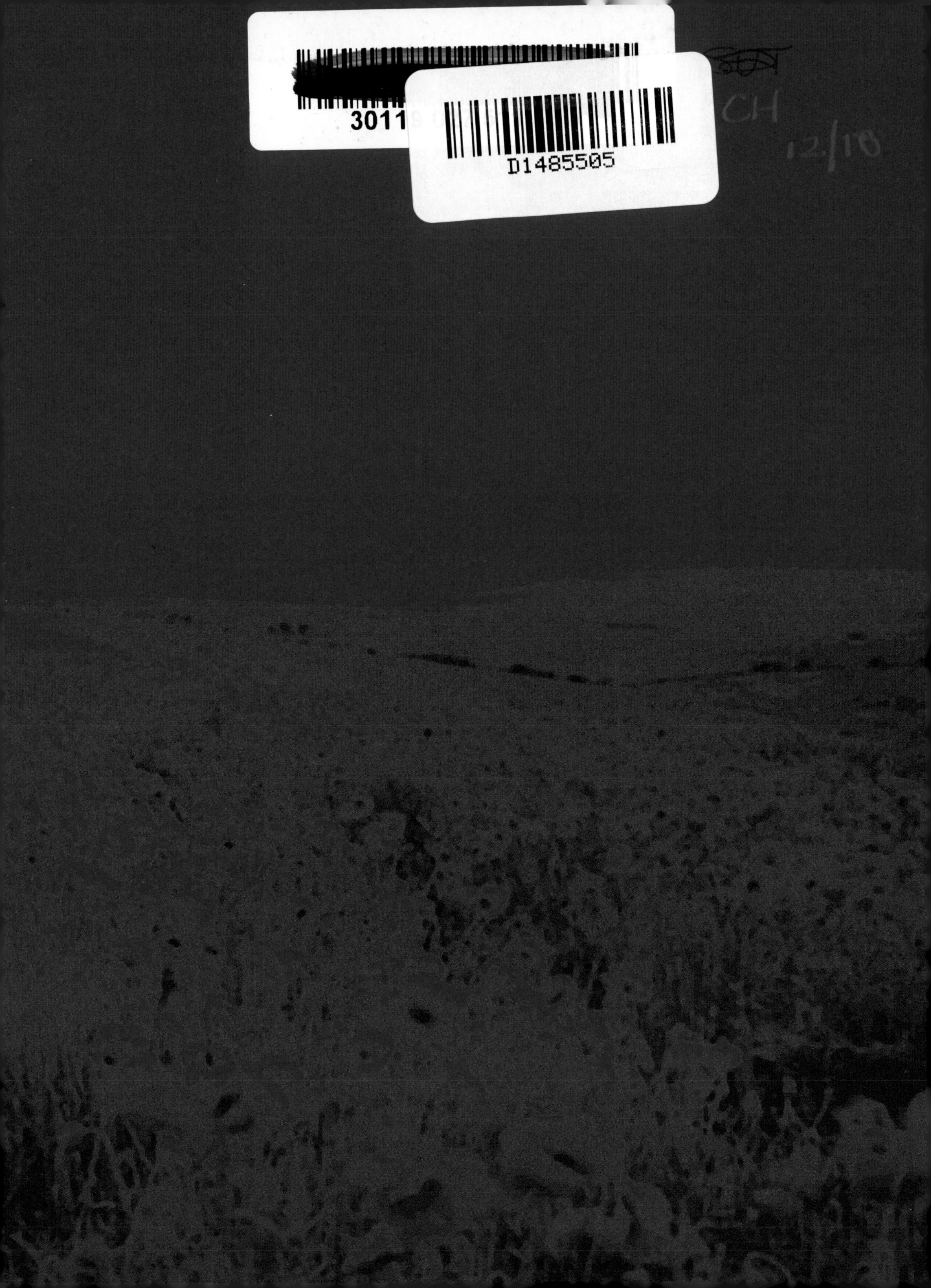

WILFRED OWEN

An Illustrated Life

WILFRED OWEN

An Illustrated Life

JANE POTTER

Bodleian Library
UNIVERSITY OF OXFORD

To Peter and Elizabeth Owen

First published in 2014 by the Bodleian Library, Broad Street, Oxford OX1 3BG
www.bodleianbookshop.co.uk
ISBN: 978 1 85124 394 5

Foreword © Jon Stallworthy, 2014
Text © Jane Potter, 2014
All images, unless specified above © Bodleian Library, University of Oxford, 2014

Excerpts from Wilfred Owen, *Selected Letters* (ed. John Bell) and Harold Owen, *Journey from Obscurity* are reprinted by permission of Oxford University Press.

Designed and typeset by Dot Little at the Bodleian Library in 10.5/14 pt Monotype Baskerville.
Printed on 120 gsm Ambergraphic by Grafos SA, Barcelona.

British Library Catalogue in Publishing Data
A CIP record of this publication is available from the British Library

CONTENTS

FOREWORD

On his last New Year's Eve, Wilfred Owen reviewed his life, writing to his mother:

> I am not dissatisfied with my years. Everything has been done in bouts:
>
> Bouts of awful labour at Shrewsbury & Bordeaux; bouts of amazing pleasure in the Pyrenees, and play at Craiglockhart; bouts of religion at Dunsden; bouts of horrible danger on the Somme; bouts of poetry always; of your affection always; of sympathy for the oppressed always.
>
> I go out of this year a Poet, my dear Mother, as which I did not enter it. I am held peer by the Georgians; I am a poet's poet.

A disciple of John Keats, the quintessential poet's poet, Owen would himself become the poet's poet of Auden and Spender in the 1930s, of Douglas and Lewis in the 1940s, of Heaney and Hughes in the 1960s. By then, of course, the poets' admiration of Owen was widely shared by poetry readers across the English-speaking world. In 1963 his voice crossed the frontiers of that world to become truly international. Making the journey, he travelled not on his own passport but that of Benjamin Britten, the text of whose *War Requiem* included nine of Owen's poems. A new and expanded edition of his *Collected Poems* was published to coincide with the launch of Decca's two-disc set of the *Requiem* that, in its first year, sold 200,000 copies and made the national poet's poet also an international poet.

The interwoven story of Owen's life and work has hitherto been told mainly by men, who have sometimes seen him as a misogynist interested only in men. Co-editor of a Penguin selection of Gurney's, Rosenberg's and Owen's poems and editor of the new edition of Owen's *Selected Letters*,

Jane Potter offers a more nuanced view of the poet's poet. At the heart of this is the most important relationship of his short life, that with his mother (to whom 554 of his 673 surviving letters are addressed). Potter's unequalled familiarity with Owen's letters enables her to see the warmth and wit his mother would have enjoyed and some of his more solemn biographers have overlooked. After a bout 'of horrible danger on the Somme', he tells her, 'I had the heavenly-dictated order to proceed on a Transport Course. Me in Transports? Aren't you?' To understand what the devout churchgoing Susan Owen would have understood, one needs to hear both the resonance of that heavenly dictation and the echo of the hymn mother and son would so often have sung together:

> Thou spread'st a table in my sight:
>   Thy unction grace bestoweth:
> And O what transport of delight
>   From thy pure chalice floweth.

('The King of Love my Shepherd is')

The flowing lines of Jane Potter's well-proportioned portrait, fleshed out with more and better photographs – many of them from the rich archive at the English Faculty Library in the University of Oxford – than any previous study of Owen's life and work, offer an ideal introduction to them both.

Jon Stallworthy
Wolfson College, Oxford

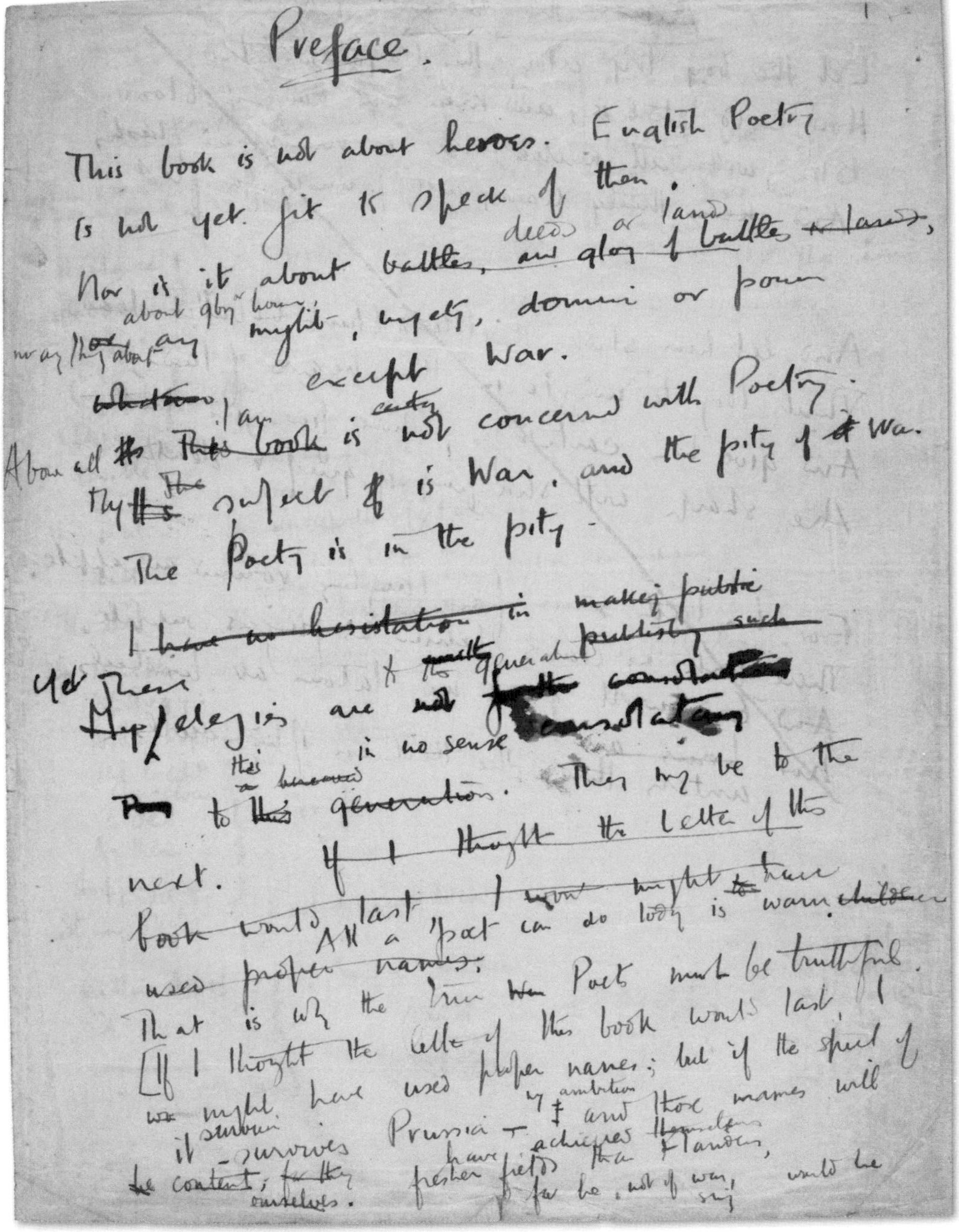

Preface.

This book is not about heroes. English Poetry
is not yet fit to speak of them.
Nor is it about deeds, or lands, nor anything about glory, honour, might, majesty, dominion or power,
except War.

Above all I am not concerned with Poetry.
The subject of it is War, and the pity of War.
The Poetry is in the pity.

Yet these elegies are to this generation in no sense consolatory. They may be to the
next. All a poet can do today is warn. That is why the true Poets must be truthful.

If I thought the letter of this book would last, I
might have used proper names; but if the spirit of
it survives Prussia, — my ambition and those names will
be content; for they will have achieved themselves fresher fields than Flanders, . . .

Figure 1 Wilfred Owen's draft Preface to his planned volume of poems, May 1918.

PREFACE

On Tuesday morning, 22 October 1918, Wilfred Owen wrote to his mother:

> Your last letter before going to Alpenrose, & the one from
> Alpenrose and the parcel reached me together yesterday. Two
> days ago I was thinking a great deal of your Restoration to
> health, and even managed to mention it, I believe! This is fine
> news of your visit to Dr. Armitage. Let nothing waver you from
> your treatment, however incommodious to other people (or
> yourself.) How happily I think of you always in bed. About the
> end of November you will start to move about your room. Your
> room must be arranged. All my Articles of Vertue which you
> like are to represent me there. My Jacobean Chest; (why not?)
> my carpets; my tall candlesticks; my pictures; my tables: have
> them all in.
>
> About Christmas you will start the hardening processes.
> You will lengthen your walks and your paces. You will grow
> keen with the keenness of frost and cold, blue sunlight. So you
> will be ready, early in February, for my Leave. We will walk to
> Haughmond, and while you are resting on the top, I will run
> round the Wrekin and back, to warm my feet.[1]

This tender letter is all the more poignant since Owen would not live to see
his next leave and walk with his mother to Haughmond Hill. In less than
two weeks he would be dead, killed on the banks of the Sambre–Oise canal
near the village of Ors in northern France, on 4 November. As the church
bells in Shrewsbury pealed out news of the Armistice on the 11th, his parents
received the telegram announcing his death. He was 25 years old.

In his short life, and in particular in his final two years, he produced poetry which shaped the twentieth century's cultural memory of the Great War, and which, in the twenty-first century, continues to have lasting resonance. In one of English literature's most famous manifestos, a draft preface to a volume of poetry he had been planning (figure 1), Owen declared, 'My subject is War and the Pity of War. The Poetry is in the pity.' Thus, he has become the poet of pity, the voice of the soldier maimed, blinded, traumatised and killed, not just in the First World War but in all wars since. Yet Owen the Poet was not made by the war. His powerful poetry reached its apotheosis in 1917–1918 only after years of literary apprenticeship, as a favoured child, a studious adolescent and a soul-searching young man.

CHAPTER 1

1893–1910

Childhood and young adulthood Oswestry, Birkenhead, Shrewsbury

Figure 2 Susan Owen with her baby son Wilfred aged 6½ months.

Figure 3 Wilfred Owen sitting on his mother's lap next to his grandfather Edward Shaw, Plas Wilmot, Oswestry, 1895. Emma Gunston is standing left next to the house maid. The children at the front are Gordon, Dorothy and Vera Gunston.

WILFRED EDWARD SALTER OWEN was born to Susan and Tom Owen on 18 March 1893 at Plas Wilmot, the Oswestry home of his maternal grandfather Edward Shaw. The six-bedroomed, creeper-covered villa, maintained by house-maids, a cook, gardener, and a gardener's boy, was built by Shaw's father-in-law, Edward Salter, in 1830. Shaw himself owned an ironmongery business and when he married Salter's daughter Mary in 1857, he acquired the substantial property. Successively town councillor, mayor, justice of the peace, and in addition being appointed to other civic duties, Edward Shaw was the epitome of Victorian respectability and success. His children, Mary (May), Emma, Edward and (Harriett) Susan were looked after by nurses and governesses.

Tom Owen, born in 1862 in Nantwich, had a very different early life, as the son of William Owen, a tailor, and his wife Martha. Cheerful, energetic and a keen reader (something he would hand down to his eldest son), at 15 Tom joined the Great Western Railway as a junior railway clerk and was posted to Oswestry. Here he met Edward Shaw (junior) at a local cricket club, both of them being keen sportsmen. Through him Tom was introduced to Susan. At 18, on 23 September 1880, Tom sailed for India on the SS *Benalder* as an ordinary seaman. Arriving in Bombay, he took his discharge certificate from the ship on 21 October and joined the Great Indian Peninsular Railway as a clerk in the Traffic Manager's Office at Bori Bunder, Bombay. During his four years in India, in which he became a member of the local militia, the GIPR Volunteer Rifles and the sailing club, he and Susan wrote to each other frequently. In 1884 he fell dangerously ill with 'some tropical fever or disease',[2] and after some months in hospital returned to England, his dream of settling in India ended. He resumed life as a railway clerk with the London & North Western and Great Western Joint Railways. By contrast, Susan's brother Edward had gone from high-spirited young man to an adult with

Figure 4 Wilfred Owen as a baby at Plas Wilmot.

Figure 5 Tom and Susan Owen with their first born son.

drinking and gambling problems, both of which had got out of hand. Susan often had to put him into bed when he came home drunk. He left England somewhere between 1888 and 1890/91 and was last known to have been in Denver, Colorado, in 1893. On 8 December 1891 Susan, dressed in mourning for her mother, who had died on 29 November, married Tom and both attempted to save Plas Wilmot through sensible economies. Amid a garden featuring mulberry, walnut and weeping ash trees, a croquet lawn, and an orchard, an idyllic life was maintained, and it was into this that Wilfred Owen was born, followed on 30 May 1896 by his sister Mary. Tom Owen's 'sea-fever' never left him, something which can be discerned in a model ship, the SS *Susan*, that he lovingly crafted for his son (figures 7, 8).

Figure 6 A lock of Wilfred Owen's hair, with a label by Susan, indicative of her hopes for him: 'The hair of Sir Wilfred Edward Salter-Owen at the age of 11½ months in the year 1894.'

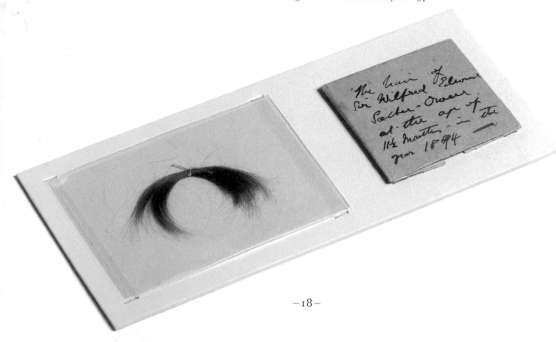

Figure 7 Wilfred Owen with the model boat made for him by his father.
Figure 8 Model boat by Tom Owen.

Figure 9 *left* The tiny soldier at Plas Wilmot.
Figure 10 *above* The tiny soldier in the Hussar uniform made for him by his mother.

Figure 11 *above* Wilfred Owen as a boy, at Plas Wilmot.
Figure 12 *right* Wilfred Owen with his siblings Harold, Mary and Colin, *c.* 1902.

The death of Edward Shaw senior from a stroke in 1897 signalled a change in fortune that forever haunted the Owen family. At the reading of the will, it was revealed that the situation was far worse than feared, and Plas Wilmot had to be sold. It was auctioned on 16 March 1897, with the family retaining only a few items of silver, linen, small furnishings and pictures, and their warm memories of a more gracious way of life.

Tom Owen moved his family to Birkenhead briefly, then obtained a temporary post at Shrewsbury where, on 5 September 1897, Harold Owen was born in a small house in Canon Street. In 1900 Tom was reappointed to Birkenhead as stationmaster at Woodside. Thus followed a number of years where house moves were a feature of family life: 7 Elm Grove in Higher Tranmere, where Colin Owen was born on 24 July 1900; then 14 Willmer Road; and finally 51 Milton Road. Harold Owen's memories of his childhood were summed up in his recollection of moving to Birkenhead:

> I was being unloaded from a dark and dripping cab on to a black wet pavement in a dank and evil-smelling street outside one of a long line of small, squalid, and near-slum dwellings. … When we had groped our way into the house, and my father made a light, the floor and walls of the passage and the small room leading from it appeared to surge and lift as if covered with a simmering treacle. We had been welcomed to our new home by armies of black beetles … . I was immediately and very violently sick, and the last impression I had before consciousness once again drifted away from me, was of Wilfred's protective rush towards me, the feel of his arms around me, and the fearful sight of the racing heaving black mass of beetles converging upon what I had thrown up.[3]

In June 1900, Wilfred Owen began to attend the Birkenhead Institute, founded in 1889 by the philanthropist George Atkin. At just over 7 years old, Wilfred was a hard-working pupil and a voracious reader. He stood rather

Figure 13 Susan Owen and her children (l–r): Colin, Mary, Harold and Wilfred, *c.* 1902.

apart from his contemporaries, and his closest friend at this time was Alec Paton, whom he met in September 1902. That November Wilfred began attending Sunday School at the evangelical Christ Church, run by the charismatic Canon W.H.F. Robson. Susan and her eldest son read the Bible together, making notes on daily Scripture reading, a practice Wilfred kept up for years. At this time, Tom Owen began to oversee classes at the Sunday School, but was rather more inclined to tell tales of the sea, sailors and foreign lands than preach the Gospel.

Indeed the contrast between Susan's personality and Tom's as well as the relationship each had with their eldest son could not have been more marked, though their mutual love was never in doubt. Susan was strictly evangelical, with a firm belief in a Divine Will. Possessive of her first-born son, Susan's relationship with Wilfred was extremely, intensely close. His religiosity was instilled by her, his obsession with his health mirrored her own. Susan passed her tendency to hypochondria on to her son, with their letters demonstrating their often obsessive concern with aches, pains and minor ailments.

Their love for each other was absolute, if at times Wilfred felt smothered – and Tom excluded – by it. His love for his father, his delight in his companionship, however, shine forth in his letters, though their number to

Figure 14a One of Wilfred Owen's schoolbooks from the Birkenhead Institute, *c.* 1908.

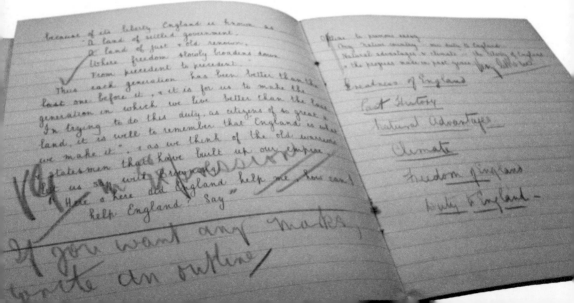

him alone is eclipsed by the over 550 letters written to Susan. Tom passed on his love of literature to his eldest son, for, an avid bookman himself, Tom would read aloud nightly to the family from Dickens, Bunyan, Stevenson and others. He also had, as Harold recalled, a 'Welsh passion for music of any sort', invented games and taught his children to swim. What became known in the family as 'Wilfred's Church' was symbolic both of his mother's hopes for him – she made all the accoutrements needed for a church service, including a mitre – and his father's penchant for theatricality:

> At first it was all very simple but as his enthusiasm grew and his imagination took wing, it became more and more elaborate . . . . Wilfred would spend a long time arranging the room, after which he would robe himself and, looking very priestlike in his surplice and mitre, would call us in to form the congregation. He would then conduct a complete evening service with remarkable exactitude and would end by reading a short sermon he had prepared with great care and thought.[4]

Tom was not often a member of this little congregation, but he 'was not antagonistic'. The practice was, according to Harold, phased out in light of 'Wilfred's mounting demands for more embellishment and I think my mother feared it might develop into Popery.'[5] Wilfred's 'schoolmasterly attitude' towards his siblings was partly the result of Susan's poor health when he was young, which left him in charge. Harold recounted frequent instances of his elder brother's heavy-handed or aloof treatment, but he recognized their distinct personalities. Whereas Harold was energetic, often combative, and considered a 'bruiser', he could only think of Wilfred 'even when he was only eleven or twelve dressed in school clothes with a schoolboy satchel on his back – as a student':

> he never ran counter to authority. This is largely explained by his natural extreme gentleness of manner – there was about

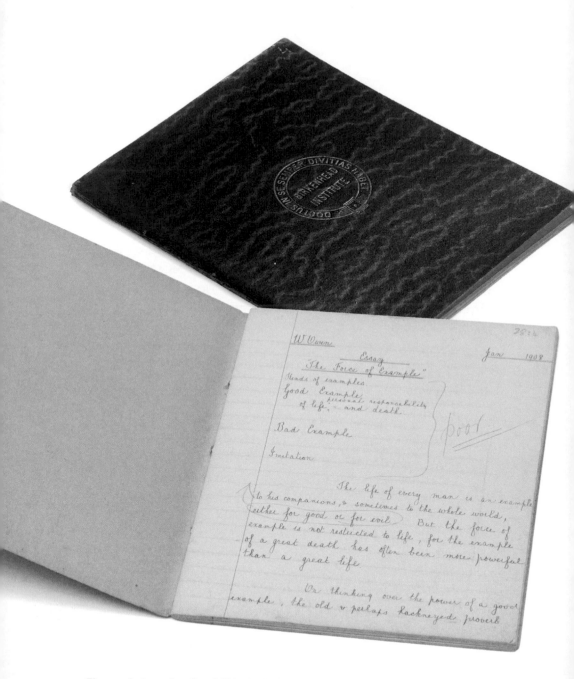

Figure 14b A page from Owen's Birkenhead schoolbook. The now-famous poet was not always a model student.

him, as well, ... something [of] ... an assured diffidence. This gravity of approach, which remained always in advance of his years, coupled as it was with his attractive appearance (not to be confused with good looks), his thick dark brown hair and small delicacy of build – perhaps a lack of robustness even – gave him an air of over-adultness. I always think of it as his 'small dark look'.[6]

Family holidays punctuated the Birkenhead years, some taken with cousins, others at the hospitality of friends in Edinburgh, Scarborough, Wimbledon and Torquay (figure 15). On one of these holidays, the student became a poet. In 1904 the family borrowed a cottage from a family friend:

It was in Broxton among the ferns and bracken and the little hills, secure in the safety and understanding love that my mother wrapped about him with such tender ministration, that the poetry in Wilfred, with gentle pushings, without hurt, began to bud, and not on the battlefields of France.[7]

This passage, like many others in *Journey from Obscurity* (1963–1965), shows that it was not only the elder Owen who had a facility with language, the ability to create poignant memory in words.

In the autumn, Wilfred moved up to the Senior School at the Birkenhead Institute and 'the role of serious student suited him well': the 'burden of homework', 'long and untidy' hair, and his tendency to lateness made him seem 'driven'.[8] He excelled in English and French, and did reasonably well in science but poorly in mathematics. At the Speech Day in 1905 he shared the prizes with Alec Paton and in 1906 he won four £5 Duke of Westminster scholarships, which saved his father two terms' worth of fees.

In 1907 Tom was appointed assistant superintendent of the Joint Railways in Shrewsbury, and for a brief time the family lived with Tom's parents at 2 Hawthorn Villas, moving to their own home, 1 Cleveland Place, Underdale

Figure 15 The Owen family on Scarborough beach, 1905.

Road, nearby. In the spring of that year, Wilfred entered Shrewsbury Borough Technical School, which doubled as a local probationer teaching college.

Although Susan was an enthusiastic member of St Julian's Church in Shrewsbury, the Temperance League and the British and Foreign Bible Society, the family – mainly at the urging of Tom, who disliked pious, over-enthusiastic clergymen – increasingly gravitated to the small church of Holy Trinity at Uffington. It was a short ferry ride across the river and, in one of his most evocative memories, Harold described a summer evening walk on the way home from Uffington:

> I had fallen back behind the others as I was sometimes wont to do – I was fond of slowly dragging my feet through the cool wetness of the grass. When I was climbing over the stile leading into the lane I noticed in the half-darkness that my boots looked strange and peering more closely I saw that they were completely covered with buttercup petals; in the darkness they glowed like gold. I was immediately intrigued with this and called out to the others that I had feet of gold, but they were a long way up the lane ... I heard Wilfred walking back to see what I was calling to them about. When Wilfred reached me he too was fascinated with the strange luminous effect. While we were still looking at them we heard my father's footsteps turn and come towards us. He was softly calling out as he came to ask if we were all right and I was just about to call back through the darkness when Wilfred gently pressed my arm for silence – hesitated a moment and then called quietly back, 'Harold's boots are blessed with gold'.[9]

This memory has been identified by Harold and others as one of the influences behind lines in the poem 'Spring Offensive': 'And the far valley behind, where the buttercup / Had blessed with gold their slow boots coming up.'

At 16, it seemed that Owen 'enjoyed the company of his contemporaries less than the contemplation of the long dead'.[10] However, he had some friends, and had a particularly strong bond with his cousins Leslie (figure 16) and Vera Gunston, with whom he formed the Astronomical, Geological and Botanical Society. It was in the letter announcing the rules of the society that Owen seems to have used his monogram for the first time, one he would later engrave on his cigarette case (figure 35). Such interests led him to a fascination with archaeology and he made numerous visits to the Roman city of Uriconium at Wroxeter, east of Shrewsbury, as well as to Silchester, near his cousins' house at Reading.

Figure 16 Owen's cousin, Leslie Gunston, as a boy.

In a letter of August 1910, he delighted in recalling a visit to 'a great geologist and collector of prehistoric implements', at Twyford:

> I have never seen in museum or house such a magnificent collection. Hardly less interesting was the mighty range of books on Geology, History, etc. And Mr. Treacher himself, with his long grey hair, philosophical manner, and dirty old coat, was a character I would go a long way to see. Hearing I was interested in Roman remains, he took me round to a shed and fished out

a small sack. 'You can have all this pottery from Silchester,' he said … . I knew it contained treasures – whether I smelt or heard, or felt or tasted them I cannot say, but I <u>knew</u>![11]

The family's new home at 71 Monkmoor Road, which Tom christened Mahim in honour of his days in India, provided this budding archaeologist and poet with a top-floor room, an eyrie, where he could have 'quietness and seclusion'.[12] But much like his own later enthusiastic admirers, Owen liked to follow in the footsteps of his favourite poets. On holiday in Torquay in the summer of 1910, he visited Coleridge's granddaughter Christabel. She and her brother Ernest Hartley Coleridge both signed Wilfred's copy of *The Golden Book of Coleridge*. In April 1911 he made what he called 'a pilgrimage to Teignmouth', where Keats lived for a time in 1818. Discovering the house, he 'gaped at it (regardless of the people in the window who finally became quite alarmed, I fancy) – to my heart's content'.[13] The visit inspired 'Sonnet: Written at Teignmouth, on a Pilgrimage to Keats's House', its sestet not only demonstrating his studied imitation, but prefiguring the language and mood of later, more mature poems:

> Eternally may sad waves wail his death,
> Choke in their grief 'mongst rocks where he has lain,
> Or heave in silence, yearning with hushed breath,
> While mournfully trail the slow-moved mists and
>   rain,
> And softly the small drops slide from weeping trees,
> Quivering in anguish to the sobbing breeze.

Back in Shrewsbury, where the sonnet was revised, he joined Wyle Cop School as a temporary pupil teacher, but was unsettled by the prospect of being a schoolmaster. The admonition of a family friend, Mrs Timpany, against the profession must have unsettled him further: 'she thinks it "wicked" that young people should enter it without a fair premonition of the

hopelessness of their fate, and without knowing of the profound dissatisfaction among all who are now teachers.'[14] At 18, Owen was wondering what he should do:

> Really, indecision is rapidly turning into distraction. When I begin to eliminate from my list all those professions which are impossible (seemingly) from a financial point of view, and then those which I feel disinclined for – it leaves nothing. But is my inclination to matter after all? Yet what I do find so hard is to distinguish between is aimlessly drifting, and waiting upon God.[15]

Figure 17 The young pupil-teacher, *c.* 1910.

CHAPTER 2

1911–1915

The search for a profession
Dunsden, Bordeaux, the
Pyrenees, Mérignac

Figure 18 *p.36* Wilfred Owen reading in the Vicarage garden at Dunsden, aged 19.

OWEN HAD ALWAYS hoped to go to university, but he needed to obtain a scholarship. Oxford was his dream, as he wrote with some bitterness but even more sadness to his cousin Leslie: 'Couldn't you divine why "Oxford" is a banned word with me. Because it is one of my most terrible regrets. I ought to be there.'[16]

The University of London's external degree was a more realistic option, and he embarked on a course of private study for the Matriculation Exam with the help of the Cambridge-based University Correspondence College. Although he passed the matriculation exam, it was not with the first-class honours he required for the scholarship. His brother recalled:

> His actual receiving of the news imprinted itself very vividly on my mind. I think my mother must have been away from home, otherwise it could not have fallen to my lot to deliver the fateful letter to him. As it was, I rushed up to his bedroom with the embossed and sealed letter – to find him, as usual, buried deep under the blankets, only the fringe of his dark hair showing from the top of his head and stupefied with over-tired sleep.
>
> My excited shout about the news I bore stabbed him awake. He sprang up in bed and snatched the thick creamy envelope from my hand and then commenced – again to use his own words – an ecstasy of fumbling, for he was trembling and shivering violently and his hands were all mixed up with the bedclothes and the envelope was obstinate and refused to open. At last he had the letter out and I shall always remember the few seconds of stillness, and then the long dragged out sigh of disappointment, despairing in its melancholy, and his inert slumping back on to the bed and the burrowing under the blankets.[17]

Figure 19 The Reverend Herbert Wigan.
Figure 20 *p. 40* Wilfred Owen in the
Vicarage garden, Dunsden, 1911.

With his hopes for university dashed, he accepted the offer from the
Reverend Herbert Wigan (figure 19) to become his unpaid lay assistant in
the parish of Dunsden, near his cousins the Gunstons. This pleased Susan
in particular, as she nurtured hopes of a career in the Church for her
eldest son. Her belief that 'God will provide' could be said to have been
realized. In exchange for help with parish work, Owen was given board and
lodging, and promised tuition from Wigan to help prepare him for another
university entrance exam. On 20 October 1911 Wigan met Owen at Reading
Station and together they travelled back to the labyrinthine vicarage built in
1870. Owen's bedroom was on the first floor and he described his 'mode of
life' to Susan:

> At seven every morning a meek voice announces to the noble
> sir that his shaving water waits outside … . At the stroke of the
> awe-inspiring gong, he takes a large chair on one side of the fire,
> in the dining room, with Mr. Kemp on the other, the Vicar at
> the table, and the domestics sitting in respectful admiration in
> a row at the end of the room. After prayers the said admiring
> domestics withdraw, and breakfast is taken … .
>
> Left alone, and with something of my gravity thrown off, I
> then set to work at a bureau-bookcase in the dining room till
> lunch. This afternoon the Vicar took me with him visiting, till
> afternoon tea. Then dinner at 7.30, of such things as jugged
> hare![18]

'Mr. Kemp' was the other lay assistant, Alfred Saxelby-Kemp, with whom
Owen became good friends. Kemp too was attempting to enter university, but
he had failed twice previously to win a scholarship. Parish work dominated
Owen's time. In addition to visiting the sick, he conducted children's services
and Scripture Union meetings, and found that 'I enjoy speaking very much.
I use no notes, and spend no great time in preparation; but I use no high
falutin' words, but try to express myself in simple, straightforward English'
without, he says 'displaying my own bumptiousness'.[19] He delighted in the
company of the young in the village, whom he referred to as 'my children'.
He was especially attached to 12-year-old Vivian Rampton, a bright boy to
whom he gave piano lessons and encouraged to read and enjoy books. He
wrote to Susan on 5 March 1912 how 'On Sat. I secretly met with Vivian at a
stile and went [on] a delicious ramble; lay in hawthorn glades, where antlered
stags would come within a few yards of us. He read to me, and I told him
tales. I took some figs of Mary's for him.'[20]

The relationship was an emotionally significant one for Owen, one he
could share with his mother but not with Wigan who – with his strict sense
of propriety and his distanced attitude towards the members of the parish
– would have found such a friendship unsuitable. And the vicar's academic

coaching left Owen wanting. No great lover of literature, Wigan offered to teach Greek and Hebrew, 'all Theological dustiness', Owen wrote: 'All my recent excursions into such fields proves it to be a shifting, hypothetical, doubt-fostering, dusty and unprofitable study.'[21] As an alternative, Owen attended botany classes at University College, Reading and found in Miss Edith Morley, head of English, a sympathetic encourager of his writing and his passion for literature, which at times was physical, nearly overwhelming. Reading Rossetti's *Life of Keats*, he felt himself 'more than once' turning 'hot and cold and trembly over the first haemorrhage scene; and sobbed over Severn's "He is gone … ." … Rossetti guided my groping hand right into the wound, and I touched, for one moment the incandescent Heart of Keats.'[22]

The poems he was composing at this time owe much to the sensuousness learned from Keats as Owen negotiated his own burgeoning sexuality. 'Lines Written on My Nineteenth Birthday' (sent in a letter to his mother on 19 March 1912), 'The Time was Aeon' and 'Ballad of a Morose Afternoon', for instance, show an intense, sensual, sometimes masochistic engagement with the human body, often the male body. Such poems lay the foundation for Owen's mature work where lips, eyes, hands, limbs are dominant images, often ravished and defiled by the violence of war. At the same time as he was exploring the visceral/visual effects that language could communicate, he discovered the aural effect of pararhyme, later used so masterfully in 'Strange Meeting'. In his copy of John Addington Symonds' biography of Shelley, Owen (who was delighted to learn that the poet lived nearby and, like him, visited the poor and the sick), amongst other annotations, marked up a series of six lines, linking in pen the words 'tomb' and 'home', 'spirit' and 'inherit', 'thou' and 'below', with their characteristic 'falling', consonantal rhymes that mirror a melancholy mood.

Yet whatever distractions his writing and reading may have offered, the grinding poverty of many in Dunsden weighed more heavily each day. His sympathy and pity for the poor were inspired by the stark contrast between their depravation and the comforts of the vicarage as well as the genteel society among which the vicar moved. Appalled, Owen wrote to his sister

Figure 21 The family on holiday at the home of Susan's old friend from Oswestry Nelly Bulman, Kelso, Scotland, 1912.

Mary about 'the wretched hovels', 'the crazy, evil-smelling huts' in which 'scores' of people 'have passed their whole lives'. Some are content with 'the Hope of a Future World', but others, 'like the beasts, have no such Hope, pass their old age shrouded with an inward gloom … deadening them to all thoughts of delight'.[23] This misfortune was becoming more and more difficult to reconcile: 'I am increasingly liberalising and liberating my thought', he wrote.[24] His participation at the 1912 Evangelical Summer Convention at Keswick and the on-going revival in the parish did nothing but speed that process. The double funeral of Alice Mary Allen and her 4-year-old daughter Hilda Agnes on 15 October prompted the poem 'Deep under Turfy Grass', in which he declares:

> I, weeping not, as others, but heart-wild,
> Affirmed to Heaven that even Love's fierce flame
> Must fail beneath the chill of this cold shame.

Such compassionate yet unflinching response 'would characterize his writings from the western front'.[25]

By December Owen's 'nerves' were 'in a shocking state'.[26] The stress of parish work, the disparity between vicarage and village life, the increasing frustration with organized evangelical religion, and the turmoil of emotions that came with emerging maturity, all seem to have reached fever-pitch. His handwriting is visibly shaky and unsettled in his letters to his mother and his sister as he catalogues how he suffers from palpitations, vertigo, indigestion and insomnia. In one letter to Mary he includes a cartoon of himself overcome by dizziness. What is described rather cryptically in his letters as a 'furor' leads to his finally revealing the true state of his spiritual and religious feelings, and both young man and vicar agree that the post had become untenable. What the 'furor' was exactly is difficult to know. It was potentially a combination of Owen's resistance to the revival and to Wigan's discovery that Owen had smuggled Vivian into the vicarage for tea. Dominic Hibberd notes that 'Wilfred's departure from Dunsden has sometimes been misrepresented', but there was 'certainly no sort of scandal', for he was received warmly by both the parishioners and Wigan himself on subsequent visits.[27] Enough, though, was enough. He needed then to 'Escape from this hotbed of religion': 'Murder will out, and I have murdered my false creed. If a true one exists, I shall find it. If not, adieu to the still falser creeds that hold the hearts of nearly all my fellow men.'[28]

On the verge of, but not actually experiencing, a nervous breakdown and suffering from congestion of the lungs, he returned to Shrewsbury in February 1913. In April Owen went to convalesce with friends in Torquay and made another pilgrimage to Teignmouth. He sat the scholarship exam for University College, Reading in July but failed. Continuing to suffer from bronchial attacks (no doubt exacerbated by his mother's insistence that he was prone to tuberculosis), he was advised by his doctor that the warmer climate of southern France might do him good. Owen took up the offer of a post as part-time English teacher with the Berlitz School in Bordeaux in mid-September, with a small allowance from his father to help cover the shortfall of his salary; as Jon Stallworthy has noted, 'Over the next two years he grew to love France and had reached perhaps the highest point of happiness that life would offer him'.[29]

Owen first found a small room to rent in Rue Castelmoron for 1 franc per day, but this proving too expensive, he soon moved to cheaper lodgings at 95 Rue Porte-Dijeaux. His workload was heavy but, while his letters to his mother catalogue a series of minor ailments, he did not regret 'having come to France'. He revelled in various fêtes in the city, including the *Bal des étudiants* and *Carnival*:

> I had huge success with my Costume: Nothing more elaborate
> than my Gown on my back a laurel wreath on my head, & a
> palm branch in the hand. These 3, (with of course a <u>Mask</u> – my
> own home-made domino) made an imposing combination! I
> was with a student (whom I like very much), & his friends. The
> crowds were enormous, & I was twice choked with confetti.[30]

Owen was offered the opportunity by M. Langholz, the sub-director of the Berlitz School, to become director of a small Berlitz business in Angers in northern France, but he would have to raise the capital and the prospect of approaching 'a rich uncle', in the Owens' case, Edward Quayle, did not sit well with either Wilfred or his father. Moreover, as Wilfred wrote to Tom, 'I have no false ideas of Business. "Anything we do to make money is Business"', but he realized that 'once fixed in a low-level Rut one is ever-after straightened there'.[31] Yet he was also not 'under any delusions as to Literature as a means of livelihood'.[32] In the end, the school was sold to someone else but Owen was not upset: 'I am glad I am not tethered to it.'[33]

The letters of the Bordeaux years are filled with his thoughts on his eventual profession, of what he would do with his life, and Tom worried about his lack of direction. M. Peyronnet, a manufacturer of perfumes, attempted to 'convert' Owen to business by offering him a job as one of his commercial travellers, but while he undertook some work for Peyronnet, he wrote to Susan that 'I could never conscientiously work hard and wholeheartedly at a business'. It would be 'a literal losing of my soul'.[34] The profession of poetry is what he is called to, the 'only one field in which I could work willingly, and would work without wage'.[35]

In addition to pouring out his feelings to his mother about a role in life, Owen's letters frequently attempt to quell her fears about the influence of French women:

> If you knew what hands have been laid on my arm, in the night, along the Bordeaux streets, or what eyes play upon me in the restaurant where I daily eat, methinks you would wish that the star and adoration of my life had risen; or would quickly rise.
>
> But never fear: thank Home, and Poetry, and the FORCE behind both. And rejoice with me that a calmer time has come for me; and that fifty blandishments cannot move me like ten notes of a violin or a line of Keats.

All women, without exception, <u>annoy</u> me, and the
mercenaries (which the innocent old pastor thought might
allure) I utterly detest; more indeed than as a charitable being,
I ought.[36]

He was not immune to feminine charms or unaware of his own
attractiveness to women, however. During a visit to Castelnau with his
close friend Raoul Lem at Easter 1914, he was the object of young Henriette
Poitou's interest – 'her marvellous eyes looked in my direction, enough
to count four times per minute' – and vies with Raoul for her attention.
Henriette appeared to prefer the young Englishman:

> we walked arm in arm. I could scarcely have been happier.
> <u>Raoul</u> might clearly have been happier than he was; but it was
> hardly <u>my</u> fault. And the memory of those moments will remain
> sweet to me, chiefly, my dear Sister, chiefly because I took no
> <u>advantage</u> of that young and ardent nature ...[37]

Another young girl – and her mother – would find Owen an attractive
companion and teacher, for that summer Owen took up the post of tutor to
Madame Léger and her daughter Nénette at Villa Lorenzo, near Bagnères-de-
Bigorre in the La Gailleste valley at the foot of the Pyrenees (figure 22). Much
younger than her husband M. Léger, who had trained as an engineer but gave
up the profession for the arts, Madame was 'elegant rather than *belle* ... [with]
shapely features luxuriant coiffure, but is much too thin to be pretty'.[38] Owen
has to calm his mother's fears about Mme Léger and her intentions:

> I am conscious that she has a considerable liking for me, both in
> a physical and intellectual sense. She is now equally conscious
> that the former liking is not reciprocated – not one little bit –
> and continues to like me for my mind's nature. If it were not so,
> – I should hop it, immejit.[39]

Figure 22 The Villa Lorenzo, *c.* 1914.

Nénette makes her tutor 'immensely happy': she is 'perfectly a child, and with that, is almost a perfect child … As far as I can judge, she has also more than her share of intellect.'[40] She declares that *'Monsieur Owen est très-joli garçon, n'est-ce-pas?'*[41] and he depicts her in his poem 'The Sleeping Beauty' as the 'marvellous Beauty', 'the fair Child', from whom he 'drew back tiptoe':

> Because it was too soon, and not my part,
> To start voluptuous pulses in her heart,
> And kiss her to the world of Consciousness.

Such innocent beauty stood in stark contrast to the war that had begun to rage in Europe. By the time Owen was fully ensconced at Villa Lorenzo at the beginning of August, Bagnères was overcome by the news: 'Women were weeping all about; work was suspended. Nearly all the men have already departed.' Because he looked French, he was the object of stares for not being in uniform. He 'had to declare myself, and get a permit to remain here; where I must stay still under penalty of arrest and sentence as a spy – unless I get a special visa for emigrating'.[42] Despite everything, he continued 'to be immensely happy and famously well'.[43] He immersed himself in French literature and through the Légers was introduced to one of the three living poets who was to have an significant influence on his work, Laurent Tailhade (the others being Harold Monro in 1915–1916 and Siegfried Sassoon in 1917).[44] A member of the Decadent School of French literature, Tailhade guided him to the work of Paul Verlaine, Gustave Flaubert and others of late-nineteenth-century Aestheticism, and its offshoots Decadence and Symbolism. Tailhade himself was smitten with the young man (figures 24, 25). When Owen called at his hotel one morning, the 'charming old gentleman'

> received me like a lover. To use an expression of the Rev. H.
> Wigan's, he quite slobbered over me. I know not how many
> times he squeezed my hand; and sitting me down on a sofa,
> pressed my head against his shoulder … . It was not intellectual;

Figure 23 *pp.50-51* Listening to a reading by Laurent Tailhade: Wilfred Owen (second from left) seated in the front row next to Mme Léger and Nénette Léger (in white) at the Casino, Bagnères-de-Bigorre, August 1914.

Figure 24 *left* The French poet Laurent Tailhade.
Figure 25 *above* Wilfred Owen and Laurent Tailhade, 1914.

Figure 26 A card inscribed to Wilfred Owen *son vieil ami* (his old friend) Laurent Tailhade, 14 September 1914.

> but I felt the living verve of the poet … who has fought <u>seventeen duels</u> (so it is said).[45]

Owen's reaction to this 'slobbering' is interesting, not only because he did not hide the event from his mother, but because he communicated it with a sense of sophistication, a knowingness about the nature of Tailhade's affection ('he received me like a lover', 'it was not intellectual'), and perhaps most importantly with a seeming lack of intimidation or concern. The nervous and delicate lay assistant had become a more confident and self-assured young man. And, as the war carried on around him, he wrote to Susan how it 'affects me less than it ought'. Echoing the degeneration debates that were a feature of the early years of the twentieth century, Owen argued:

> I can do no service to anybody by agitating for news or making dole over the slaughter. On the contrary I adopt the perfect English custom of dealing with an offender: a Frenchman duels

with him: an Englishman ignores him. I feel my own life all the more precious and more dear in the presence of this deflowering of Europe. While it is true that the guns will effect a little useful weeding, I am furious with chagrin to think that the Minds which were to have excelled the civilization of ten thousand years, are being annihilated – and bodies, the product of aeons of Natural Selection, melted down to pay for political statues. I regret the mortality of the English regulars less than that of the French, Belgian, or even Russian or German armies: because the former are all Tommy Atkins, poor fellows, while the continental armies are inclusive of the finest brains and temperaments of the land. There is no exception made but for the diseased, the imbecile, and the criminal.[46]

The poet of pity is absent in this passage and when he tells Harold about a visit to a war hospital, graphic description and accompanying illustrations are almost more voyeuristic than pleading. He also pompously declared, 'I deliberately tell you all this to educate you to the actualities of the war.'[47]

Nevertheless, he was not unaffected by the rhetoric of the press:

The *Daily Mail* speaks very movingly about the 'duties shirked' by English young men. I suffer a good deal of shame. But while those ten thousand lusty louts go on playing football I shall go on playing with my little axiom: – that my life is worth more than my death to Englishmen.

Do you know what would hold me together on a battlefield?:
The sense that I was perpetuating the language in which Keats
and the rest of them wrote![48]

The many indecisions of 1914–1915 found Owen considering joining the
French army or the Italian army, then deciding on the Artists' Rifles: 'I don't
want the bore of training, I don't want to wear khaki; nor yet to save my
honour before inquisitive grand-children fifty years hence. But I now do most
intensely want to fight.'[49]

In September he returned to Bordeaux, residing briefly with the
Légers, and once Madame departed on a business trip for Canada (on
which she had hoped he might accompany her), he moved first to the Lems,
then to a room at Chez Veuve Martin, 31 rue Desfourniels. He attended
free university courses and tutored his own pupils. In December Mlle de
la Touche offered him the post of tutor to her two nephews, English boys,
Johnny and Bobbie at Mérignac (figure 28). He was to 'look after the boys in
the afternoons; terms mutual; and I to keep up as many Bordeaux lessons as
I wish, tramming or bicycling in every morning. We should work two hours
a day; and amuse ourselves the rest.'[50] The boys were meant to return to
their public school, Downside, but the threat of submarines in the Channel
continually delayed their leaving. In May 1915 Owen travelled to London on
business for M. Peyronnet, representing him at the British Industries Fair.
While in London, he attended a talk at Guildhall sponsored by the Central
Committee for Patriotic Organizations, at which Kipling was present. After
a brief visit to Shrewsbury and Mahim, he returned to Bordeaux. His lessons
with the boys continued through the summer of 1915, but by September
the decision was finally made to send the boys back to Downside. On 14
September Owen left Bordeaux with Johnny and Bobbie, staying overnight
in London before seeing them off to their school and returning himself to
Shrewsbury for a month. In mid-October he travelled to Reading to visit his
cousins before going on to London on 20 October to enlist.

Figure 27 *p.55* A statue of Hermes bought by Owen possibly in Bordeaux. It was given to Leslie Gunston after Owen's death.

Figure 28 *above* Wilfred Owen and the family group at Mérignac, summer 1915. In the back row, left to right, are the daughter of neighbour Admiral Castéjas, Charles, Johnny and Bobbie de la Touche, Owen, David de la Touche. At the front, Mlle Puységur, an invalid who lived at the chalet, Mlle Anne de la Touche (seated in white holding a teapot) and Admiral Castéjas's son.

CHAPTER 3

1915–1916

Enlistment and training
London, Romford, Aldershot

I AM the British Army! Three of us had to read the Oath
together; the others were horribly nervous! and read the wrong
Paragraph until the Captain stopped them! 'Kiss the Book!'
says Captain. One gives it a tender little kiss; the other a loud
smacking one!!'[51]

Owen found lodgings at a French boarding house, Les Lilas, 54 Tavistock
Square, a short walk from the Artists' Rifles Headquarters in Duke's
Road. During his three-and-a-half day sick leave, given as the result of his
typhoid inoculation, he is glad he '<u>did</u> put up in a Boarding House, not in a
Bedroom without meals or attention!',[52] justifying the expense of 35 shillings
per week. He felt 'at home in the region', too, having stayed in Bloomsbury
before on his previous trips. 'Wadded in fog' and pervaded by 'ghostly
aristocracy', the area for him is indicative of why 'In London I cannot be
unhappy.' In contrast to what he called the 'dismally forlorn' and 'detestably
sordid' atmosphere of other cities, London has an air of the 'Mysterious',
of being 'romantically free and easy; what elsewhere seems old dinginess
is here suggestive Antiquity'.[53] This affinity with the capital no doubt was
due to its literary associations. The British Museum, where he had seen
Keats's manuscripts on display as a young student, was nearby and Dickens
lived in Tavistock House opposite the square in the 1850s. Another site of
importance for Owen was the Poetry Bookshop, at 35 Devonshire Street off
Theobald's Road, run by Harold Monro, editor of *The Poetry Review*. During
that October he attended poetry readings there, once speaking afterwards
to Monro himself. His days were spent at drill – 'It is really no great strain
to strut round the gardens of a West-end square for six or seven hours a day',
and he found he enjoyed wearing his uniform, echoing much of the patriotic
propaganda that abounded on posters and in popular novels about the

change in men who don khaki : 'Walking abroad, one is the admiration of all little boys, and meets an approving glance from every eye of eld.'[54] Monro, however, 'smiled sadly at my khaki' when Owen returned to the Poetry Bookshop for a reading of work of the Indian poet Rabindrinath Tagore.[55] Knowing Monro's poetry well, Owen was attuned to the affinity between the bookseller's reaction to seeing him in uniform and Monro's recent poem 'Youth in Arms', in which the speaker addresses a 'happy boy', who in his 'modern avatar' he 'hardly recognised'. Echoes of Owen's own later subjects are heard in the stanza:

> Greybeards plotted. They were sad.
> Death was in their wrinkled eyes.
> At their tables, with their maps
> Plans and calculations, wise
> They all seemed; for well they knew
> How ungrudgingly Youth dies.

It was thus not only the reduction in rent that delighted Owen when he:

> found a room at 5/6 per week, right opposite the Poetry
> Bookshop!!
> A plain enough affair – candlelight – no bath – and so on;
> but there is a coffee-shop underneath.[56]

He planned to move once he'd settled his bills at Tavistock Square. However, he didn't have long to enjoy the new lodgings as he was soon posted to Hare Hall Camp, Gidea Park, Romford, Essex, exchanging 'the comfort of his candle-lit room for a rowdy barrack hut'.[57] He got on 'splendidly well', regardless of this and the often punishing schedule of training: 'holding rifles frozen over with snow all day was ghastly',[58] he wrote. Orderly duties led him to declare to Leslie Gunston (figure 30), that he 'never thought myself capable of such strenuosity as to do skivvy's drudgery from 6.30 a.m. to 6.30

Figure 29 *pp.58–59* Wilfred Owen with the 5th Manchesters at Witley Camp, 1916.

Figure 30 *left* Leslie Gunston as an adult.

Figure 31 *right* Postcard from Wilfred Owen to Leslie Gunston, 28 November, 1915.

p.m.!'[59] (figure 31). Despite not getting leave for Christmas, he reassured Susan that 'We shall have a merry time even in the Hut, and I am sure you will like to know I am in the bosom of a family at dinner-time!'[60] He was invited by one of the Boy Scouts at the camp, Raymond Williams, whose family (two girls, two boys) took 'pleasure in inviting and feasting soldiers'.[61]

In the New Year he refused the offer of a commission with the Lancashire Fusiliers, who were about to embark for France, because he had not yet finished his musketry course. By the end of February Owen was back in

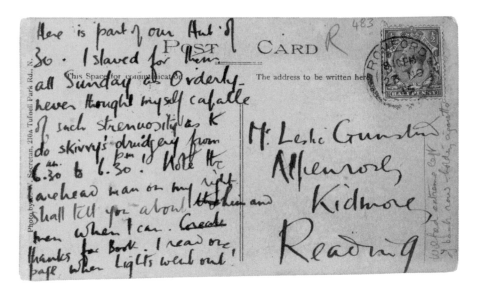

London on a ten-day course – 'Lectures nearly all day, on Gas, Horses, Bombs, and such objects'[62] – and 'like a homing pigeon',[63] he made his way to the Poetry Bookshop, renting an attic room at the top. On his final night he was able to share his work, mainly sonnets, with Monro:

> I have the time of my life. For he was 'very struck' with these sonnets. He went over the things in detail and he told me what was fresh and clever, and what was second-hand and banal; and what Keatsian, and what 'modern'.
>
> He summed up their value as far above that of the Little Books of Georgian Verse.[64]

Returning to Romford, he was assigned to Balgores House for Officers' School, where 'another 8 weeks of schooling … started in earnest': 'eternal inspections, parades, inspections, punishment parades, & more inspections'.[65]

Figure 32 Portrait of Wilfred Owen 5th Manchesters, 1916.

The caricature of the colonel 'cursing us from the top of a Golf Mound' is pure Owen: '[He] drills us, foaming at the mouth. Sometimes he follows at our heels, barking like a collie after straggling sheep.' The Coldstream Guard Sergeant 'abuses us in bad English and worse Language'.[66] But he achieved his marks in his exams taken in April with 'high and very high marks in Musketry, Reconnaissance, and Drill – full marks for Drill – But in Military Law I came pretty low!'[67]

On 4 June 1916 he was gazetted as 2nd Lieutenant, 5th Battalion the Manchester Regiment, and joined Milford Camp near Witley,

Figure 33 Wilfred Owen, civilian clothes, side view, seated. Photograph by John Gunston, *c.* 1915.

Surrey, two weeks later. (figure 32) Musketry courses found him to be a first-class shot. During a visit to the Gunstons at Kidmore End in July, his uncle John took the now famous photographic portraits of the new officer, with his 'dark eyes and faint Gioconda-like smile'[68] (cover image / frontispiece). In mid-August he returned to Shrewsbury on leave. An application for transfer to the Royal Flying Corps came to nothing, but Owen told his mother he had no regrets. Harold's visit to him in camp in September 1916 finds him a mature, confident infantry officer, in stark contrast to the awkward, young cadet of earlier visits:

> Gone was our everlasting brotherliness, it had disappeared
> on that warm summery afternoon; in its place came enjoyment
> and appreciation; we could relish one another as persons. In

Wilfred I could find no sign of raillery, no sardonic comment, no critical depreciation of me. His eyes were clear of their usual film of intolerant misunderstanding, they remained grave without being sombre, and jumping out from the gravity now and again would come that twinkling naughtiness, a spontaneous burst of gaiety as we laughed together. His eyes looked deeper and calmer – completely calm – the superficial look of strained irritability was no longer in them. I could sense that he was at ease with himself.[69]

  Throughout the autumn he was posted variously to Oswestry, Southport ('the most unsatisfactory sea-side place in Europe), and Fleetwood, where he was officer in charge of Brigade Firing Point. 'Engrossed' in his work with 'a good deal of writing in the evenings', Owen enjoyed his 'good times' there, and was not pleased with the 'bitter change' back to Southport in early December, where he was 'stuck on the new Musketry Party, firing at Crossens, where we march out every morning, about 3 miles, starting at 7.15.'[70] He found his commandant, Major Melville, 'a snotty, acid, scot, impatient, irritated wretch'.[71] Christmas, though, was spent at Mahim on embarkation leave. He had been given orders to proceed to Folkestone for France.

Figure 34 *far left* Wilfred Owen in uniform. Photograph by John Gunston, *c.* 1915.

Figure 35 *left* Wilfred Owen's cigarette case inscribed with his monogram.

Figure 36 *above* Owen's binoculars.

Dulce et Decorum est.

Bent double, like old beggars under sacks,

Knock-kneed, coughing like hags, we cursed through sludge,

Till on the haunting flares we turned our backs

And towards our distant rest began the trudge.

~~Some~~ New marched asleep. ~~Many~~ had lost their boots

But limped on, blood-shod. All went lame; all blind;

~~Deaf even~~ Drunk with fatigue; deaf even to the hoots

Of ~~tired, outstripped Five-Nines~~ that dropped behind.
 ~~gas shells~~
 gas shells ~~dropping soft~~

Then somewhere near in front: Whew...fup, fop, fup,

Gas. shells? ~~Or~~ duds? We loosened masks in case,—

And listen~~ed~~. ~~Nothing~~. Far ~~no~~ rumouring of Krupp.

Then ~~sudden~~ poisons ~~but us~~ ~~stung~~ in the face.
 ~~crept~~ Sudden

Gas! GAS! Quick, boys! — An ecstasy of fumbling,

Fitting the clumsy helmets just in time;

But someone still was yelling out and stumbling,

And flound'ring like a man in fire or lime ...

Dim, through the misty panes and thick green light,

As under a green sea, I saw him drowning.

In all my dreams, before my helpless sight,

He plunges at me, guttering, choking, drowning.

CHAPTER 4

1917

Active service and shell shock
The Somme and Craiglockhart

Figure 37 Manuscript page of 'Dulce et Decorum Est', 1918. The earliest surviving manuscript is dated 'Oct. 8, 1917', but Owen revised the poem between January and March 1918, probably at Scarborough but possibly at Ripon.

'THERE IS A FINE heroic feeling about being in France, and I am in perfect spirits', Wilfred wrote to Susan on New Year's Day 1917.[72] Shortly afterwards – having joined his regiment, the 2nd Manchesters, at Halloy, near Beaumont Hamel, which had just been involved in severe fighting – his tone had changed:

> we were let down, gently, into the real thing, Mud.
>
> It has penetrated now into that Sanctuary my sleeping bag, and that holy of holies my pyjamas. For I sleep on a stone floor and the servant squashed mud on all my belongings; I suppose by way of baptism. We are 3 officers in this 'Room', the rest of the house is occupied by servants and the band; the roughest set of knaves I have ever been herded with. Even now their vile language is shaking the flimsy door between the rooms. …
>
> On all the officers' faces there is a harassed look that I have never seen before, and which in England, never will be seen – out of jails. The men are just as Bairnsfather has them – expressionless lumps. …
>
> I am perfectly well and strong, but unthinkably dirty and squalid.[73]

This was the worst winter of the war, a grim year on the Western Front.

His letters from this time are as evocative, shocking and profoundly moving as any of the poetry that his experiences inspired. More immediate and raw, they demonstrate Owen's powers of vivid description, of cadence and sounds, and the slow accretion of detail that marks his most famous poems. As Douglas Kerr demonstrates in his study *Wilfred Owen's Voices* (1993), the language of his evangelical religious upbringing, of the Romantics, of French Decadents and Symbolists, and of the army into which he had so quickly been inducted all come into play in powerful and striking ways.

When he heard the clamour of the guns for the first time, on 7 January at Beauval, he called it 'a sound not without a certain sublimity', but he

> must not disguise from you the fact that we are at the one of the
> worst parts of the Line. ...
> I can't tell you any more Facts. I have no Fancies and no
> Feelings.
> Positively they went numb with my feet.[74]

Moving forward by motor-bus to Betrancourt with the 2nd Manchesters on 8 January, he encounters 'a Gehenna' in which 'There is a terrific Strafe on. Our artillery are doing a 48 hours bombardment. At night it is like a stupendous thunderstorm, for the flashes are quite as bright as lightning.' His 'new chosen and faithful Servant discovered a fine little hut' in which to billet, but 'There is only one disadvantage: there is a Howitzer just 70 or 80 yards away, firing over the top every minute or so.'[75] In this atmosphere of 'mud and thunder', he is

> transformed now, wearing a steel helmet, buff jerkin of leather,
> rubber-waders up to the hips, & gauntlets. But for the rifle,
> we are exactly like Cromwellian Troopers. The waders are
> of course indispensable. In 2½ miles of trench which I waded
> yesterday there was not one inch of dry ground. There is a mean
> depth of 2 feet of water.[76]

On 12 January he led his platoon to the front to hold a dug-out in No Man's Land at Beaumont Hamel:

> I can see no excuse for deceiving you about these last 4 days.
> I have suffered seventh hell.
> I have not been at the front.

I have been in front of it.

I held an advanced post, that is, a 'dug-out' in the middle of No Man's Land.

We had a march of 3 miles over shelled road then nearly 3 along a flooded trench. After that we came to where the trenches had been blown flat out and had to go over the top. It was of course dark, too dark, and the ground was not mud, not sloppy mud, but an octopus of sucking clay, 3, 4, and 5 feet deep, relieved only by craters full of water. Men have been known to drown in them. Many stuck in the mud & only got on by leaving their waders, equipment, and in some cases their clothes.

High explosives were dropping all around us, and machine guns spluttered every few minutes. But it was so dark that even the German flares did not reveal us.

Three quarters dead, I mean each of us 3/4 dead, we reached the dug-out, and relieved the wretches therein. I then had to go forth and find another dug-out for a still more advanced post where I left 18 bombers. I was responsible for other posts on the left but there was a junior officer in charge.

My dug-out held 25 men tight packed. Water filled it to a depth of 1 or 2 feet, leaving say 4 feet of air.

One entrance had been blown in & blocked.

So far, the other remained.

The Germans knew we were staying there and decided we shouldn't.

Those fifty hours were the agony of my happy life.

Every ten minutes on Sunday afternoon seemed an hour.

I nearly broke down and let myself drown in the water that was now slowly rising over my knees.

Towards 6 o'clock, when, I suppose, you would be going to church, the shelling grew less intense and less accurate: so that I was mercifully helped to do my duty and crawl, wade, climb and flounder over No Man's Land to visit my other post. It took me half an hour to move about 150 yards.

I was chiefly annoyed by our own machine guns from behind. The seeng-seeng-seeng of the bullets reminded me of Mary's canary. On the whole I can support the canary better.

In the Platoon on my left the sentries over the dug-out were blown to nothing. One of these poor fellows was my first servant whom I rejected. If I had kept him he would have lived, for servants don't do Sentry Duty. I kept my own sentries half way down the stairs during the more terrific bombardment. In spite of this one lad was blown down and, I am afraid, blinded.[77]

It is the source of his poem 'The Sentry', with a shocking and brilliant switch of pronoun:

> We dredged it up, for dead, until he whined,
> 'O sir – my eyes, – I'm blind, – I'm blind, – I'm blind.'
> Coaxing, I held a flame against his lids
> And said if he could see the least blurred light
> He was not blind; in time they'd get all right.
> 'I can't,' he sobbed. Eyeballs, huge-bulged like squids',
> Watch my dreams still, –

By 19 January Owen and his men were 'a long way back in a ruined village, all huddled together in a farm … . Snow is deep about, and melts through the gaping roof, on to my blanket. We are wretched beyond my previous imagination – but safe.'[78] The night before, he 'had to "go up" with a party', which 'got lost in the snow':

> I went on ahead to scout – foolishly alone – and when, half a
> mile away from the party, got overtaken by
> GAS

WILFRED OWEN: AN ILLUSTRATED LIFE

It was only tear-gas from a shell, and I got safely back (to the
party) in my helmet, with nothing worse than a severe fright!
And a few tears, some natural, some unnatural.[79]

The off-setting and upper-casing of the word 'GAS' echoes what later
became arguably Owen's most famous poem, 'Dulce et Decorum Est' (figure
37), with its exclamation: 'Gas! GAS! Quick, boys! – An ecstasy of fumbling,
/ Fitting the clumsy helmets just in time'.

Cataloguing the worsening conditions, he declared: 'They want to call
No Man's Land "England" because we keep supremacy there', but

It is like the eternal place of gnashing of teeth; the Slough of
Despond could be contained in one of its crater-holes; the fires of
Sodom and Gomorrah could not light a candle to it – to find the
way to Babylon the Fallen.

It is pock-mocked like a body of foulest disease and its odour
is the breath of cancer.

I have not seen any dead. I have done worse. In the dank
air I have perceived it, and in the darkness, felt. Those 'Somme
Pictures' are the laughing stock of the army – like the trenches
on exhibition in Kensington.

No Man's Land under snow is like the face of the moon chaotic,
crater-ridden, uninhabitable, awful, the abode of madness.[80]

In the midst of this building-up of horror, this unforgettable sequence of
words, Owen's black humour peeks through: 'To call it "England"! I would
as soon call my House (!) Krupp Villa, or my child Chlorina-Phosgena.'[81]

Reprieve from all this came in the form of a course on Transport Duties
in February at Abbeville, where he was elected mess president. When it
ended on 25 February, it took him nearly a week to reach his battalion dug-
out headquarters at Bouchoir, 18 miles south-east of Amiens, where he was
posted to B-Company under the command of Captain Sorrel:

I am ever so happy to be with him. He chokes filthiness as
summarily as I ever heard a Captain do, or try to do. He is
himself an aesthete ...

He seems to be one of the few young men who live up to my
principle: that Amusement is never an excuse for 'immorality',
but that Passion may be so.[82]

On 13/14 March he fell into 'a kind of well', hitting his head on the way
down. He was trapped for three days, and emerged with concussion. He was
sent to the 13th Casualty Clearing Station at Gailly on the Somme Canal and
discharged at the end of March to rejoin his battalion at St Quentin. He was
then transferred to A Company under the command of 2nd Lt Taylor. On 14
April at Savy Wood, A Company led the attack 'and of course lost a certain
number of men. I had some extraordinary escapes from shells & bullets. ...
Never before has the Battalion encountered such intense shelling as rained
on us as we advanced in the open.'[83] Thirty men were killed in the barrage.
'Spring Offensive' was Owen's poetic rendering. He was in the line for twelve
days:

I think the worst incident was one wet night when we lay up
against a railway embankment. A big shell lit on the top of the
bank, just 2 yards from my head. Before I awoke, I was blown
into the air right away from the bank! I passed most of the
following days in a railway Cutting, in a hole just big enough to
lie in, and covered with corrugated iron. My brother officer of B
Coy, 2/Lt Gaukroger lay opposite in a similar hole. But he was
covered with earth, and no relief will ever relieve him, nor will
his Rest will be a 9 days-Rest.[84]

While on a rest period in Quivieres, he was observed by the commanding
officer, Lt Col. Luxmoore, to be behaving strangely. He was sent on 2 May to
the 13th Casualty Clearing Station:

The Doctor suddenly was moved to forbid me to go into action next time the Battalion go, … he is nervous about my nerves, and sent me down yesterday – labelled Neurasthenia. … Do not for a moment suppose I have had a 'breakdown'. I am simply <u>avoiding</u> one.[85]

To Colin he wrote, with a kind of *Boy's Own Paper* enthusiasm overlaying the real danger, later rendered in 'The Show':

The sensations of going over the top are about as exhilarating as those dreams of falling over a precipice, when you see the

Figure 38 Craiglockhart Military Hospital, Edinburgh in 2008. Only the façade survives of the building that is now Napier University. A different view may be seen in a contemporary 1917 photo in figure 40.

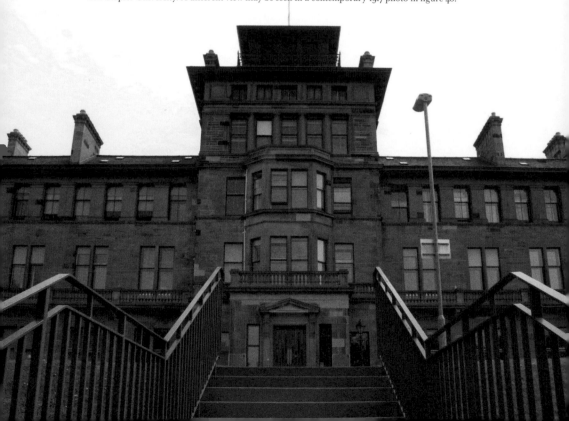

rocks at the bottom surging up to you. I woke up without being squashed. Some didn't. There was an extraordinary exultation in the act of slowly walking forward, showing ourselves openly.

There was no bugle and no drum for which I was very sorry. I kept up a kind of chanting sing-song: Keep the Line straight!

Not so fast on the left!

Steady on the Left!

Not so fast!

Then we were caught in a Tornado of Shells. The various 'waves' were all broken up and we carried on like a crowd moving off a cricket-field. When I looked back and saw the ground all crawling and wormy with wounded bodies, I felt no horror at all but only an immense exultation at having got through the Barrage.[86]

As in Dunsden, experience leads him to further reassessment of his religious beliefs and the sway of the established Church:

I am more and more Christian as I walk the unchristian ways of Christendom. Already I have comprehended a light which never will filter into the dogma of any national church: namely that one of Christ's essential commands was: Passivity at any price! Suffer dishonour and disgrace; but never resort to arms. Be bullied, be outraged, be killed; but do not kill. It may be a chimerical and an ignominious principle, but there it is. It can only be ignored: and I think pulpit professionals are ignoring it very skilfully and successfully indeed. ...

And am I not myself a conscientious objector with a very seared conscience? ...

Christ is literally in no man's land. There men often hear His voice: Greater love hath no man than this, that a man lay down his life – for a friend.

Is it spoken in English only and French?
I do not believe so.
    Thus you see how pure Christianity will not fit in with pure patriotism.[87]

Transferred on 11 June to No. 1 General Hospital at Étretat, he was looked after by American doctors and nurses. On 13/14 June he crossed at Le Havre and was assessed at the Welsh Hospital, Netley (the Royal Victoria Hospital), at Southampton Water. On 25 June the Medical Board assessed his 'highly strung temperament' and marked him

Figure 39 Captain A.J. Brock, RAMC, 1915. Owen was put under his care at Craiglockhart Military Hospital.

unfit for general service for six months. He was posted to Craiglockhart War Hospital in Edinburgh (figure 38).

Founded as a hydropathic establishment in 1880, by the time Owen arrived Craiglockhart had 'an air of genteel melancholy as pervasive as rising damp had entered the bones of building long before it was opened as a Military Hospital, under the Red Cross, in the summer of 1916'.[88] Owen was put in the care of Captain Arthur Brock RAMC (figure 39), a 'perceptive doctor' who 'believed shell-shock to result from broken contact with real life, and sought to re-establish that vital connection by means of "work-cure" (or, as he termed it, "ergotherapy")'.[89] Under his direction, Owen joined the field club and became editor of the hospital magazine, *The Hydra* (figures 40, 41). At Brock's suggestion he wrote 'The Wrestlers', based on the legend of

The Hydra cover (May 26 1917):

with the Editor's compliments

The HYDRA
Journal of the Craiglockhart War Hospital

No. 3 | MAY 26TH, 1917 | PRICE 6D

CONTENTS

PAGE

Editorial . . . . . 7 | The Chronicles of a V.O.S.
The Shamrock . . . . . 7 | The V.A.D.'s Lament
Notes and News . . . . 7 | Caveman and Trenchman .
The Dachshund's Lament . . 10 | A Collier's Thowts . .
Correspondence . . . . 10 | Concerts . . . .

H. & J. Pillans & Wilson, Printers, Edinburgh.

Figure 40 *The Hydra*, cover, issue for 26 May 1917.

No. 3 | NEW SERIES | January 1918

HYDRA
The MAGAZINE of CRAIGLOCKHART WAR HOSPITAL

H. & J. Pillans & Wilson, Printers, Edinburgh

Figure 41 *The Hydra*, cover, advertising issue, January 1918.

Hercules and Antaeus, an image of which
the doctor had on his office wall. Owen
gave lectures, acted in amateur dramatics
and took German lessons with Frank
Nicholson, librarian of the University of
Edinburgh. He also taught literature to
a class of thirty-nine boys at Tynecastle
Secondary School, who 'seemed most
intelligently attentive' to the uniformed
officer.[90] Family friends, the Newboults,
provided him with a comfortable off-duty
environment at their home in Leith, where
he would read poems to Mrs Newboult
and help her 14-year-old daughter with her
homework. Owen was particularly fond of

Figure 42 *left* Siegfried Sassoon. Photograph
by Bassano,1920.

Figure 43 *above* Wilfred Owen, with seven-
year-old Arthur Newboult, Leith, Edinburgh,
July 1917.

7-year-old Arthur Newboult (nicknamed 'Chubby Cubby'), for whom he wrote
the poems 'Winter Song' and 'Sweet is your Antique Body', which enshrine
and celebrate the boy's tender innocence, soon to be taken over by 'Youth' and
adulthood, when 'Your eyes shall close, being opened to the world.' Excursions
over the Pentland Hills, swimming which 'never fails to give me a Greek
feeling of energy and elemental life'; editing *The Hydra*, from which he learned
'the awful finality of a corrected proof'; and acting in the hospital production
of the play *Lucky Durham* kept him 'full of activities'. As he wrote to Susan:

> At present I am a sick man in hospital, by night; a poet, for quarter
> of an hour after breakfast; I am whatever and whomever I see while
> going down to Edinburgh on the tram: greengrocer, policeman,
> shopping lady, errand boy, paper-boy, blind man, crippled Tommy,
> bank-clerk, carter, all of these in half an hour; next a German
> student in earnest; then I either peer over the bookstalls in back-
> streets, or do a bit of a dash down Princes Street, – according as I
> have taken weak tea or strong coffee for breakfast.[91]

Figure 44a Portrait photograph of Midshipman Harold Owen.

Craiglockhart provided Owen with a crucial meeting, which would be remembered as one of the greatest and most influential friendships in literary history. Siegfried Sassoon (figure 42) arrived there on 23 July 1917, having been sent to 'Dotty-ville', as he called it, because of his outspoken statement against the war, which was published in *The Times* and read out in Parliament. To avoid a court-martial, his friends – including Robert Graves – had him diagnosed as suffering from shell shock or a nervous breakdown. Sassoon denied he had suffered either.

Owen had been reading Sassoon at the time and was

> feeling at a very high pitch of emotion. Nothing like his trench life sketches has ever been written or ever will be written. Shakespere reads vapid after these. ... I think if I had the choice of making friends with Tennyson or with Sassoon I should go to Sassoon.[92]

Mustering the courage, Owen visited his rooms as an acolyte, bringing copies of Sassoon's *The Old Huntsman and Other Poems* (1917) for him to autograph. Sassoon also read a number of Owen's poems:

> Some of my old Sonnets didn't please him at all. But the 'Antaeus' he applauded fervently; and a short lyric which I don't think you know 'Sing me at morn but only with thy Laugh' he pronounced perfect work, absolutely charming, etc. etc. and begged that I would copy it out for him, to show to the powers that be.[93]

Figure 44b Midshipman Harold Owen (standing right) and his family, 1917 (standing to his right, Colin Owen and Susan Owen; seated, Mary Owen and Tom Owen).

As Jon Stallworthy notes:

> The older poet's advice and encouragement, showing the
> younger how to channel memories of battle – recurring in
> obsessive nightmares which were a symptom of shell-shock
> – into a poem such as 'Dulce et decorum est', complemented
> Dr Brock's 'work-cure'. The final manuscript of 'Anthem for
> Doomed Youth' carries suggestions (including that of the title) in
> Sassoon's handwriting.[94]

It was the beginning of Owen's *annus mirabilis*.[95]

Owen was passed fit for military service by a medical board in October
1917. During his stay at home in Shrewsbury, he wrote to Sassoon of the
elder poet's influence on him, as 'a tiresome little knocker on your door': 'I
held you as Keats + Christ + Elijah + my Colonel + my father-confessor +
Amenophis IV in profile.' He goes on candidly, as a self-confident man, to
declare:

> In effect it is this: that I love you, dispassionately, so much, so
> <u>very</u> much, dear Fellow, that the blasting little smile you wear on
> reading this can't hurt me in the least.
>   If you consider what the above Names have severally done for
> me, you will know what you are doing. And you have <u>fixed</u> my
> Life – however short. You did not light me: I was always a mad
> comet; but you have fixed me. I spun round you a satellite for a
> month, but I shall swing out soon, a dark star in the orbit where
> you will blaze.[96]

The literary acolyte and maturing poet spent the rest of his leave in
London, where he met Robert Ross and a number of Ross's friends, including
Arnold Bennett and H.G. Wells. To Sassoon, he recalled 'a glorified morning
at the Reform, & evening at Half Moon St.'.[97] In late November he rejoined

the 5th Manchesters in Scarborough, and was stationed at the Clarence Gardens Hotel, acting as camp commandant / major domo to the officers of the 5th (Reserve) Battalion. Finding rooms for newcomers, he saw that breakfast was ready in time, undertook correspondence and inspection of rooms, ordered food from the grocers, and was also in charge of wine and tobacco. The books he read at Scarborough in the winter of 1917/18 included the English translation of Henri Barbusse's novel *Le Feu,* translated as *Under Fire: The Story of a Squad* in 1916 by William Fitzwater Wray. It was to be a significant influence on Owen's thinking and poetry, and its episodic, brutal and vivid evocations of the horrors of warfare may be seen reimagined in 'Strange Meeting', 'Miners' and 'Cramped in that Funnelled Hole'.

Having spent Christmas at Scarborough, he wrote to Susan on New Year's Eve:

> I am not dissatisfied with my years. Everything has been done in bouts:
>
> Bouts of awful labour at Shrewsbury & Bordeaux; bouts of amazing pleasure in the Pyrenees, and play at Craiglockhart; bouts of religion at Dunsden; bouts of horrible danger on the Somme; bouts of poetry always; of your affection always; of sympathy for the oppressed always.
>
> I go out of this year a Poet, my dear Mother, as which I did not enter it. I am held peer by the Georgians; I am a poet's poet.
>
> I am started. The tugs have left me; I feel the great swelling of the open sea taking my galleon.[98]

The Sentry

We'd found an old Boche dug-out, and he knew,
And gave us hell; for shell on frantic shell
Lit full on top, but never quite burst through.
Rain, guttering down in waterfalls of slime,
Kept slush waist-high and rising hour by hour,
And choked the steps too thick with clay to climb.
What murk of air remained stank old, and sour
With fumes from whizz-bangs, and the smell of men
Who'd lived there years, and left their curse in the den,
If not their corpses ...
                              There we herded from the blast
Of whizz-bangs; but one found our door at last, –
Buffeting eyes and breath, snuffing the candles,
And thud! flump! thud! down the steep steps came thumping
And sploshing in the flood, deluging muck,
The sentry's body; then his rifle, handles
Of old Boche bombs, and mud in ruck on ruck.
We dredged it up, for dead, until he whined,
'O sir – my eyes, – I'm blind, – I'm blind, – I'm blind.'
Coaxing, I held a flame against his lids
And said if he could see the least blurred light
He was not blind; in time they'd get all right.
'I can't,' he sobbed. Eyeballs, huge-bulged like squids',
Watch my dreams still, – yet I forgot him there
In posting Next for duty, and sending a scout

To beg a stretcher somewhere, and flound'ring about
To other posts under the shrieking air.

Those other wretches, how they bled and spewed,
And one who would have drowned himself for good, –
I try not to remember these things now.
Let Dread hark back for one word only: how,
Half-listening to that sentry's moans and jumps,
And the wild chattering of his shivered teeth,
Renewed most horribly whenever crumps
Pummelled the roof and slogged the air beneath, –
Through the dense din, I say, we heard him shout
'I see your lights!' – But ours had long gone out.

Dulce et Decorum Est

Bent double, like old beggars under sacks,
Knock-kneed, coughing like hags, we cursed through sludge,
Till on the haunting flares we turned our backs
And towards our distant rest began to trudge.
Men marched asleep. Many had lost their boots
But limped on, blood-shod. All went lame; all blind;
Drunk with fatigue; deaf even to the hoots
Of tired, outstripped Five-Nines that dropped behind.

Gas! GAS! Quick, boys! – An ecstasy of fumbling,
Fitting the clumsy helmets just in time;
But someone still was yelling out and stumbling,
And flound'ring like a man in fire or lime …
Dim, through the misty panes and thick green light,
As under a green sea, I saw him drowning.

In all my dreams, before my helpless sight,
He plunges at me, guttering, choking, drowning.

If in some smothering dreams you too could pace
Behind the wagon that we flung him in,
And watch the white eyes writhing in his face,
His hanging face, like a devil's sick of sin;
If you could hear, at every jolt, the blood
Come gargling from the froth-corrupted lungs,
Obscene as cancer, bitter as the cud
Of vile, incurable sores on innocent tongues, –
My friend, you would not tell with such high zest
To children ardent for some desperate glory,
The old Lie: Dulce et decorum est
Pro patria mori.

Spring Offensive

Halted against the shade of a last hill
They fed, and eased of pack-loads, were at ease;
And leaning on the nearest chest or knees
Carelessly slept.
                   But many there stood still
To face the stark blank sky beyond the ridge,
Knowing their feet had come to the end of the world.
Marvelling they stood, and watched the long grass swirled
By the May breeze, murmurous with wasp and midge;
And though the summer oozed into their veins
Like an injected drug for their bodies' pains,
Sharp on their souls hung the imminent ridge of grass,
Fearfully flashed the sky's mysterious glass.

Hour after hour they ponder the warm field
And the far valley behind, where buttercups
Had blessed with gold their slow boots coming up;
When even the little brambles would not yield
But clutched and clung to them like sorrowing arms.
They breathe like trees unstirred.

Till like a cold gust thrills the little word
At which each body and its soul begird
And tighten them for battle. No alarms
Of bugles, no high flags, no clamorous haste, —

Only a lift and flare of eyes that faced
The sun, like a friend with whom their love is done.
O larger shone that smile against the sun, –
Mightier than his whose bounty these have spurned.

So, soon they topped the hill, and raced together
Over an open stretch of herb and heather
Exposed. And instantly the whole sky burned
With fury against them; earth set sudden cups
In thousands for their blood; and the green slope
Chasmed and deepened sheer to infinite space.

Of them who running on that last high place
Breasted the surf of bullets, or went up
On the hot blast and fury of hell's upsurge,
Or plunged and fell away past this world's verge,
Some say God caught them even before they fell.

But what say such as from existence' brink
Ventured but drave too swift to sink,
The few who rushed in the body to enter hell,
And there out-fiending all its fiends and flames
With superhuman inhumanities,
Long-famous glories, immemorial shames –
And crawling slowly back, have by degrees
Regained cool peaceful air in wonder –
Why speak not they of comrades that went under?

Anthem for Doomed Youth

What passing-bells for these who die as cattle?
   – Only the monstrous anger of the guns.
   Only the stuttering rifles' rapid rattle
Can patter out their hasty orisons.
No mockeries now for them; no prayers nor bells;
   Nor any voice of mourning save the choirs, –
The shrill, demented choirs of wailing shells;
   And bugles calling for them from sad shires.

What candles may be held to speed them all?
   Not in the hands of boys but in their eyes
Shall shine the holy glimmers of goodbyes.
   The pallor of girls' brows shall be their pall;
Their flowers the tenderness of patient minds,
And each slow dusk a drawing-down of blinds.

[Cramped in that Funnelled Hole]

Cramped in that funnelled hole, they watched the dawn
Open jagged rim around; a yawn
Of death's jaws, which had all but swallowed them
Stuck in the bottom of his throat of phlegm.

They were in one of many mouths of Hell
Not seen of seers in visions; only felt
As teeth of traps; when bones and the dead are smelt
Under the mud where long ago they fell
Mixed with the sour sharp odour of the shell.

prayer of the poor man unless he is parched or faint, while he
will listen to the prayer of the rich man who has possibly
overfed.

On Sunday, January 6th, the Solemn Day of Intercession,
all the poor man's pubs. were closed by order, while the pubs. of
the rich were open.—Yours, &c.,

ELSIE F. BUCKLEY.

44, Clanricarde Gardens, W. 2.

Poetry.

MINERS.

THERE was a whispering in my hearth,
  A sigh of the coal,
Grown wistful of a former earth
  It might recall.

I listened for a tale of leaves
  And smothered ferns,
Frond-forests, and the low sly lives
  Before the fawns.

My fire might show steam-phantoms simmer
  From Time's old cauldron,
Before the birds made nests in summer,
  Or men had children.

But the coals were murmuring of their mine,
  And moans down there
Of boys that slept wry sleep, and men
  Writhing for air.

I saw white bones in the cinder-shard,
  Bones without number.
For many hearts with coal are charred,
  And few remember.

I thought of all that worked dark pits
  Of war, and died
Digging the rock where Death reputes
  Peace lies indeed:

Comforted years will sit soft-chaired,
  In rooms of amber,
The years will stretch their hands, well-cheered
  By our life's ember;

The centuries will burn rich loads
  With which we groaned,
Whose warmth shall lull their dreaming lids,
  While songs are crooned;
But they will not dream of us poor lads
  Lost in the ground.

WILFRED OWEN.

CHAPTER 5

1918

The last year
Ripon and France

WHILST STATIONED AT Scarborough, Owen read of a pit explosion at Podmore Hall Colliery, Halmerend, in which over 140 men and boys were killed. It inspired his poem 'Miners', which was published in *The Nation* on 26 January (figure 45), one of only five poems he saw in print in his lifetime. The others were 'The Next War' in *The Hydra* (29 September 1917), 'Song of Songs' in *The Hydra* (1 September 1917) and *The Bookman* (May 1918), and 'Futility' and 'Hospital Barge' in *The Nation* (15 June 1918). In the second week of March he was posted to the Northern Command Depot at Ripon. His camp in the fields west of the city was not conducive to his writing, so he rented a room at 7 Borage Lane, which he found on a walk from camp into the town.

> Outside my cottage-window children play soldiers so piercingly that I've moved up into the attic, with only a skylight. It is a jolly Retreat. There I have tea and contemplate the inwardness of war, and behave in an owlish manner generally.[99]

Here, getting physically fit and 'completely restituted from Shell Shock', he wrote and revised in that attic room his most famous poems, including 'The Send-Off', 'Insensibility', 'Strange Meeting', 'Exposure' and 'Futility'.

He spent mid-May on leave in London and took a flat in Half-Moon Street above Robert Ross's. He called his reception in London among the literary set, including Osbert Sitwell, 'magnificent', with 'more invitations to lunch & dinner than I could manage!'[100] Ross suggested he send his work to the publisher William Heinemann, for whom he was a reader:

> Judging from my own diffidence, <u>and</u> the state of the paper supply a book is not likely to appear before next Spring. I am

Army  Orders

BY
General Sir H. S. Rawlinson, Bart.
G.C.V.O., K.C.B., K.C.M.G., COMMANDING FOURTH ARMY.

MILITARY SECRETARY'S BRANCH.

IMMEDIATE REWARDS

(a) Under authority delegated by His Majesty the King, the Field-Marshal Commanding-in-Chief has made the following awards for gallantry and devotion to duty in action :—

BAR TO THE DISTINGUISHED SERVICE ORDER

Captain and Brevet Major (a/Lieutenant-Colonel) C. E. R. G. ALBAN, D.S.O., Liverpool Regiment, attached Lancashire Fusiliers.

THE DISTINGUISHED SERVICE ORDER

Major a/Lieutenant-Colonel) F. C. ALDOUS, Manchester Regiment, attached Machine Gun Corps.
Major J. L. MURPHY, Manchester Regiment.

SECOND BAR TO THE MILITARY CROSS

Second Lieutenant (a/Captain) W. KAY, M.C., Manchester Regiment.

BAR TO THE MILITARY CROSS

Lieutenant (a/Captain) L. TAYLOR, M.C., Manchester Regiment.
Temporary Lieutenant (a/Major) F. A. HOOPER, M.C., Machine Gun Corps.

THE MILITARY CROSS

Temporary-Lieutenant J. A. KILPATRICK, Royal Engineers.
Temporary Lieutenant (a/Major) E. D. MOORE, Royal Engineers.
Temporary Second Lieutenant W. OATES, Royal Engineers.
Lieutenant (a/Captain) T. RUSSELL, Royal Scots.
Lieutenant (a/Captain) P. E. TOWNEND, Lancashire Fusiliers.
Second Lieutenant H. WHITEHEAD, Lancashire Fusiliers.
Temporary Second Lieutenant C. H. J. HULTON, Lancashire Fusiliers.
Temporary Lieutenant L. P. STEPHENS, Dorsetshire Regiment.
Temporary Lieutenant B. R. COBLEY, Manchester Regiment.
Second Lieutenant W. E. S. OWEN, Manchester Regiment.
Temporary-Second Lieutenant B. BURROWS, Manchester Regiment.
Temporary Second Lieutenant J. FOULKES, Manchester Regiment.
Temporary Second Lieutenant F. JOHNSON, Manchester Regiment.
Temporary Lieutenant F. MIDDLEMISS, Highland Light Infantry.
Lieutenant R. R. S. TITCHENER, Rifle Brigade seconded Machine Gun Corps.
Temporary Lieutenant W. G. ELIAS, Machine Gun Corps.
Temporary Lieutenant T. ROBERTS, Machine Gun Corps.
Temporary Second Lieutenant G. B. MAXWELL, Machine Gun Corps.
No. 1175 Company Sergeant Major C. W. MUTTERS, D.C.M., M.M., Manchester Regiment.

THE DISTINGUISHED CONDUCT MEDAL

No. 35407 Sergeant J. DINSDALE, Royal Field Artillery.
No. 2932 Sergeant (a/Company Sergeant Major) F. CAPON, Lancashire Fusiliers.
No. 140510 Corporal W. SPENCER, Machine Gun Corps.

(b) Under authority delegated by the Field-Marshal Commanding-in-Chief, Corps Commanders have made the following awards for gallantry and devotion to duty in action :—

BAR TO THE MILITARY MEDAL

No. 235441 Private R. A. OWEN, M.M., London Regiment.
No. 497261 Sergeant J. GIBSON, M.M., Royal Army Medical Corps.

THE MILITARY MEDAL

No. 685171 Sergeant J. FORSHAWE, Royal Field Artillery.
No. 191251 Gunner J. SPENCE, Royal Field Artillery.
No 741954 Sergeant (a/Company Sergeant Major) F. N. BEAN, London Regiment.
No. 722859 Sergeant W. B. HEASMAN, London Regiment.
No. 723538 Sergeant J. SARGENT, London Regiment.
No. 722858 Lance Corporal F. G. BEAVAN, London Regiment.
No 470762 Lance Corporal P. SANKERWITZ, London Regiment.
No. 721450 Private V. HASSAN, London Regiment.
No. 423139 Private W. RODWAY, London Regiment.
No. 551936 Rifleman W. J. MILLS, London Regiment.

H. C. HOLMAN, *Major-General*,
D.A. and Q.M.G., Fourth Army.

rather proud – to have got so far on <u>one</u> published poem. Almost an unparalleled case, what![101]

New friends and acquaintances also included Charles Scott Moncrieff, whom he had met months earlier in January at Robert Graves's wedding to Nancy Nicholson – where, to his delight, he was also introduced to Edward Marsh and others 'as "Mr. Owen, Poet" or even "Owen, the poet".'[102]

Returning briefly to Ripon, he was graded fit for general service in June and reposted to Scarborough. There he received 'an urgent request from the Sitwells in London for more of my poems for their 1918 Anthology', *Wheels*: 'I want no limelight, and celebrity is the last infirmity I desire. <u>Fame is the recognition of one's peers</u>. I have already more than their recognition: I have the silent and immortal friendship of Graves and Sassoon and those.'[103] In July he began assembling the volume he called *Disabled and Other Poems*, and for which he wrote his famous manifesto, left in draft form at his death. It has become his epitaph and provides some of the most quoted phrases in literature:

> This book is not about heroes. English poetry is not yet fit to speak of them.
>
> Nor is it about deeds, or lands, nor anything about glory, honour, might, majesty, dominion, or power, except War.
>
> Above all I am not concerned with Poetry.
>
> My subject is War, and the pity of War.
>
> The Poetry is in the pity.
>
> Yet these elegies are to this generation in no sense consolatory. They may be to the next. All a poet can do today is warn. That is why the true Poets must be truthful.
>
> (If I thought the letter of this book would last, I might have used proper names; but if the spirit of it survives – survives Prussia – my ambition and those names will have achieved fresher fields than Flanders … .)[104]

Figure 46 *p.97* Army Order Publishing Wilfred Owen's Military Cross, 20 February 1919.

Figure 47 *above* Wilfred Owen, last portrait, 1918.

His final meeting with Sassoon took place in London on 15 August. After a day spent with Osbert Sitwell attending a harpsichord concert, taking tea at Sitwell's flat, conversing as they sat in Chelsea Physic Garden and having supper at the Reform Club, Owen said goodbye to his mentor and friend on the steps of the Lancaster Gate hospital, where Sassoon was recovering from a head wound. (In what Dominic Hibberd calls 'one of his "Mad Jack" adventures',[105] Sassoon was returning through No Man's Land, having thrown bombs at a German machine gun, when he was shot in the head by a British sniper, who thought he was the enemy.) Scott Moncrieff, who worked at the War Office, had been trying to get Owen a posting in England as a cadet battalion lecturer, but to no avail. Owen thus spent his week-long draft leave in Shrewsbury, and then with Susan and Colin (now a cadet in the Royal Flying Corps) in Hastings. On 26 August he was passed fit and instructed to proceed from Scarborough and report to the embarkation commandant at Folkestone. Again, he was with Susan, now for the last time. Looking out over the Channel, he quoted to her lines from Tagore: 'When I go from hence, let this be my parting word, that what I have seen is unsurpassable.'

By 9 September Owen was at the front at Amiens, and on 15 September he was assigned to D Company, where he was appointed bombing officer to his battalion. He went into action and was involved in breaking through the Beaurevoir–Fonsomme Line on 1 October – 1,400 yards of line were cleared and 210 prisoners were captured in hand-to-hand fighting. Counterattacks continued through the night: five officers were killed and six wounded, including 2nd Lt F. Potts, one of Owen's closest comrades. Eighty-five other ranks were killed or wounded. The battalion was relieved on 3 October and pulled back to dug-outs on the banks of the St Quentin Canal. In his letter of 4/5 October to his mother on his march back to Hancourt for a rest, he wrote:

> I can find no word to qualify my experiences except the word
> SHEER. (Curiously enough I find the papers talk about sheer
> fighting!) It passed the limits of my Abhorrence. I lost all my

earthly faculties, and fought like an angel.

If I started into detail of our engagement I should disturb the censor and my own Rest.

You will guess what has happened when I say I am now Commanding the Company, and in the line had a boy lance-corporal as my Sergeant-Major.

With this corporal who stuck to me and shadowed me like your prayers I captured a German Machine Gun and scores of prisoners.

I'll tell you exactly how another time. I only shot one man with my revolver (at about 30 yards!); The rest I took with a smile. The same thing happened with other parties all along the line we entered.

I have been recommended for the Military Cross; and have recommended every single N.C.O. who was with me!

My nerves are in perfect order.

I came out in order to help these boys – directly by leading them as well as an officer can; indirectly, by watching their sufferings that I may speak of them as well as a pleader can. I have done the first.

Of whose blood lies yet crimson on my shoulder where his head was – and where so lately yours was – I must not now write.[106]

To Sassoon of the same incident, the death of his 'excellent little servant Jones', he wrote a week later:

the boy by my side, shot through the head, lay on top of me, soaking my shoulder, for half an hour.

Catalogue? Photograph? Can you photograph the crimson-hot iron as it cools from the smelting? That is what Jones's blood looked like, and felt like. My senses are charred.

I shall feel again as soon as I dare, but now I must not. I don't take the cigarette out of my mouth when I write Deceased over their letters.[107]

The fragment, 'I Saw his Round Mouth's Crimson Deepen as it Fell', probably drafted at Hancourt, appears to be the working out of such feelings.

It is unlikely that Owen knew he had been awarded the MC, the citation for which reads:

> For conspicuous gallantry and devotion to duty in the attack on
> the Fonsomme Line on 1st/2nd October 1918. On the Company
> Commander becoming a casualty, he assumed command and
> showed fine leadership and resisted a heavy counter-attack.
> He personally manipulated a captured enemy machine gun in
> an isolated position and inflicted terrible losses on the enemy.
> Throughout he behaved most gallantly.

It was known that the Germans were falling back and there were rumours that Austria had surrendered. On 29 October Owen and his battalion moved into the line at St Souplet, the line west of the Sambre–Oise Canal, north of Ors, having been cleared. The next objective was to cross the canal. This was due to take place on the night of 3/4 November. On 31 October he wrote what was to be his last letter to his mother from 'The Smoky Cellar of the Forester's House' (figure 48). His vivid description of the 'inmates' is an affectionate portrait of those with whom he served:

> So thick is the smoke in this cellar that I can hardly see by a
> candle 12 ins. away, and so thick are the inmates that I can
> hardly write for pokes, nudges & jolts. On my left the Coy.
> Commander snores on a bench: other officers repose on wire
> beds behind me. At my right hand, Kellett, a delightful servant
> of A Coy. in The Old Days radiates joy & contentment from

pink cheeks and baby eyes. He laughs with a signaller, to whose left ear is glued the Receiver; but whose eyes rolling with gaiety show that he is listening with his right ear to a merry corporal, who appears at this distance away (some three feet) nothing [but] a gleam of white teeth & a wheeze of jokes.

Splashing my hand, an old soldier with a walrus moustache peels & drops potatoes into the pot. By him, Keyes, my cook, chops wood; another feeds the smoke with the damp wood.[108]

Figure 48 The Forester's House in 1992.

He happily reassures Susan that 'It is a great life. I am more oblivious than alas! yourself, dear Mother, of the ghastly glimmering of the guns outside, & the hollow crashing of the shells.' The letter (figure 49) ends with some of the most poignant words he ever wrote:

> I hope you are as warm as I am; as serene in your room as I
> am here; and that you think of me never in bed as resignedly
> as I think of you always in bed. Of this I am certain you could
> not be visited by a band of friends half so fine as surround me
> here.[109]

Zero hour for IX Corps was 5.45 a.m., 4 November. The 14th Brigade crossed the canal but the 96th Brigade, which included the 2nd Manchesters, was not successful. The engineers got a bridge across, but the area was swept with shell and machine-gun fire. Wilfred Owen was last seen walking alongside the canal, encouraging his men along the water's edge and patting them on the shoulder, saying 'You're doing very well, my boy', when he was hit and killed. The war was over just seven days later.

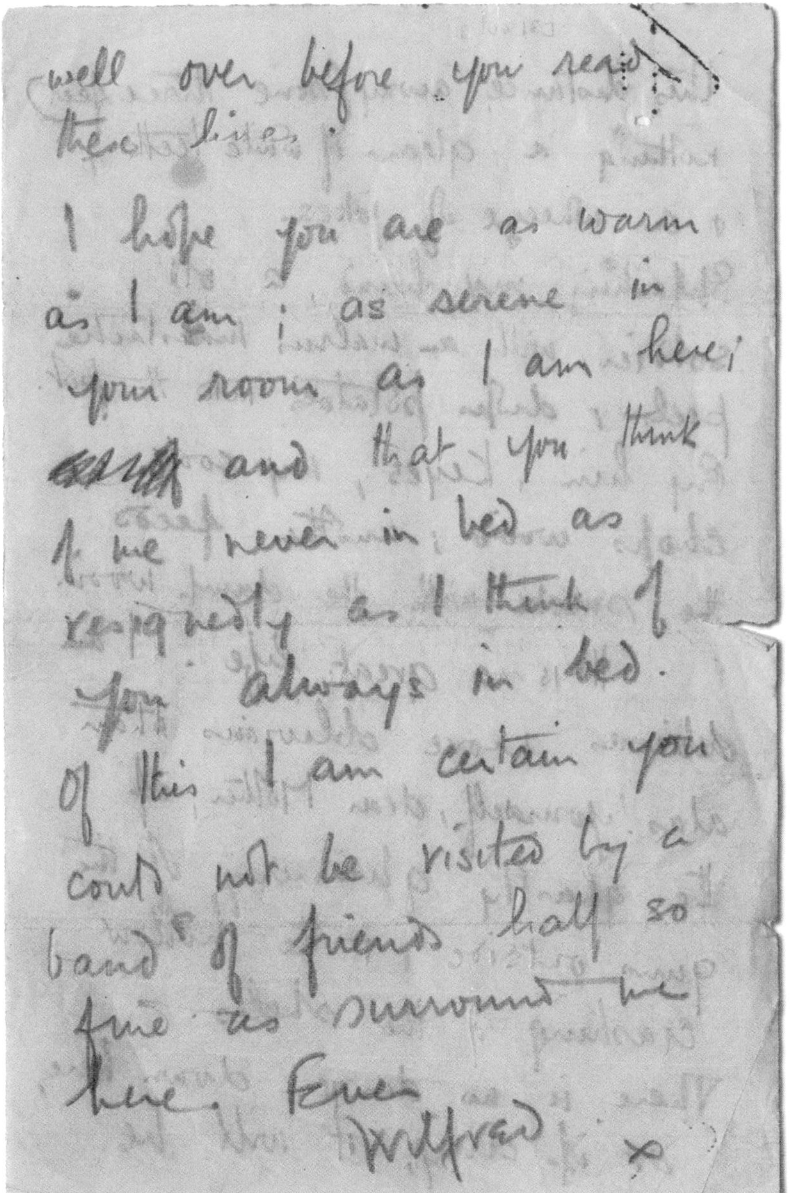

well over before you read
the~~~~ lines.

I hope you are as warm
as I am & as serene in
your room as I am here; &
~~~~ and that you think
of me never in bed as
respectedly as I think of
you always in bed.
Of this I am certain you
could not be visited by a
band of friends half so
fine as surround me
here. Ever
Wilfred x

Figure 49 Final page of Wilfred Owen's last letter to Susan Owen, 31 October 1918.

Figure 50 Front Line map from Tom Owen's scrapbook.

Figure 51 *right* 'Roll of Honour' newspaper cutting from Tom Owen's scrapbook.

ROLL OF HONOUR.

171 CASUALTIES TO OFFICERS.

64 REPORTED DEAD.

THE ARMY.

The following casualties are announced by the War Office :—

KILLED.

ANDERSON, Sec. Lt., A. D., G. Gds.

BAXTER, Sec. Lt. J. D. P., Lond. R.

CHISHOLM, Maj. E. A., M.C., R.F.A.

DODD, Sec. Lt. J. O'C., R. Muns. Fus.

ESDAILE, Capt. A. J., Devon R.

FRYER, Sec. Lt. C. J. G., M.C., Herts R.

HUDSPITH, Lt. W. L., Midd'x R.

HUNKIN, Lt. W. B. C., R. Welsh Fus.

JONES-BATEMAN, Capt. F., R. Welsh Fus.

KIRK, Sec. Lt. J., Manch. R.   **VC**

LEONARD, Sec. Lt. D., M.M., Yorks R.

LLEWELLYN, Sec. Lt. V., R. Welsh Fus.

MacINTYRE, Sec. Lt. C. F. D., R.F.A.

OWEN, Capt. M. de B., Herts R.

OWEN, Sec. Lt. W. E. S., Manch. R.   **M.C.**

PADLEY, Sec. Lt. P., R.F.A.

POWELL, Sec. Lt. W. E. G. P. W., W. Gds.

ROBINSON, Maj. F. A., M.C., Tank Corps

SHAW, Sec. Lt. W. D., R. Fus., att. Manch. R.

TROTMAN, Sec. Lt. F. H. L., Devon R.

TRYON, Maj. G. A., M.C., K.R. Rif. C.

VINCENT, Lt. A. E., R.F.A.

Previously reptd. Missing, believed Killed, now reptd. Killed.

SMITH, Sec. Lt. A. W., M.C., Gord. Highrs.

Previously reptd. Missing, now reptd. Killed.

BENNIE, Sec. Lt. A., R. Scots

CURRIE, Sec. Lt. W. G., M.C., Linc. R.

MANGER, Sec. Lt. E., M.G.C.

SMITH, Sec. Lt. T., R. Scots

DIED OF WOUNDS.

BLENKINSOP, Lt. W. M., Durh. L.I.

BLYTH, Lt. W., M.G.C.

BROCK, Lt. C. H., Devon R.

CLAPHAM, Lt. E., D. of Well. R.

EVANS, Sec. Lt. N. E., R.F.A.

FORD, Sec. Lt. D. M., Sco. Rif.

WESTCOTT, Capt. E., M.C., W. Yorks R.

Previously reptd. Wounded, now reptd. Died of Wounds.

DRAPER, Sec. Lt. J., L.N. Lan. R.

MEWSON, Sec. Lt. FitzA. R. R.F.A.

DIED.

ANDERSON, Maj. G. G., R.A.M.C.

BROAD, Maj. R. B., R.F.A.

CLEE, Lt. T. H., Worc. R., att. Lan. Fus.

HICKEY, Sec. Lt. D., Leins. R.

MEADOWCROFT, Sec. Lt. J., R.E.

PEARSON, Capt. J. S., A.S.C., att. R.G.A.

PETTIGREW, Lt. John, Spec. List, att. S. Persia Rif.

RICHARDSON, Capt. P. B., M.G.C.

SCHUH, Capt. R. O., M.C., Devon R.

WELLS, Sec. Lt. F. N., A.S.C.

WILEY, Lt. E. O. S., Durh. L.I.

WILFORD, Lt. L. E., S. Staff. R.

KILLED IN ACTION.

OWEN.—Killed in action, on the 4th Nov., 1918, in France, SEC. LIEUT. WILFRED E. S. OWEN, 5th Batt. Manchester Regiment, eldest son of Mr. and Mrs. Tom Owen, Mahim, Monkmoor-road, Shrewsbury, aged 25 years.

Miners

There was a whispering in my hearth,
 A sigh of the coal,
Grown wistful of a former earth
 It might recall.

I listened for a tale of leaves
 And smothered ferns,
Frond-forests, and the low sly lives
 Before the fauns.

My fire might show steam-phantoms simmer
 From Time's old cauldron,
Before the birds made nests in summer,
 Or men had children.

But the coals were murmuring of their mine,
 And moans down there
Of boys that slept wry sleep, and men
 Writhing for air.

And I saw white bones in the cinder-shard,
 Bones without number.
Many the muscled bodies charred,
 And few remember.

I thought of all that worked dark pits
　　Of war, and died
Digging the rock where Death reputes
　　Peace lies indeed.

Comforted years will sit soft-chaired,
　　In rooms of amber;
The years will stretch their hands, well-cheered
　　By our life's ember;

The centuries will burn rich loads
　　With which we groaned,
Whose warmth shall lull their dreaming lids,
　　While songs are crooned;
But they will not dream of us poor lads,
　　Left in the ground.

The Send-Off

Down the close darkening lanes they sang their way
To the siding-shed,
And lined the train with faces grimly gay.

Their breasts were stuck all white with wreath and spray
As men's are, dead.

Dull porters watched them, and a casual tramp
Stood staring hard,
Sorry to miss them from the upland camp.

Then, unmoved, signals nodded, and a lamp
Winked to the guard.

So secretly, like wrongs hushed-up, they went.
They were not ours:
We never heard to which front these were sent;

Nor there if they yet mock what women meant
Who gave them flowers.

Shall they return to beating of great bells
In wild train-loads?
A few, a few, too few for drums and yells,

May creep back, silent, to village wells,
Up half-known roads.

Insensibility

1

Happy are men who yet before they are killed
Can let their veins run cold.
Whom no compassion fleers
Or makes their feet
Sore on the alleys cobbled with their brothers.
The front line withers.
But they are troops who fade, not flowers,
For poets' tearful fooling:
Men, gaps for filling:
Losses, who might have fought
Longer; but no one bothers.

2

And some cease feeling
Even themselves or for themselves.
Dullness best solves
The tease and doubt of shelling,
And Chance's strange arithmetic
Comes simpler than the reckoning of their shilling.
They keep no check on armies' decimation.

3

Happy are these who lose imagination:
They have enough to carry with ammunition.
Their spirit drags no pack.
Their old wounds, save with cold, can not more ache.
Having seen all things red,
Their eyes are rid
Of the hurt of the colour of blood for ever.
And terror's first constriction over,
Their hearts remain small-drawn.
Their senses in some scorching cautery of battle
Now long since ironed,
Can laugh among the dying, unconcerned.

4

Happy the soldier home, with not a notion
How somewhere, every dawn, some men attack,
And many sighs are drained.
Happy the lad whose mind was never trained:
His days are worth forgetting more than not.
He sings along the march
Which we march taciturn, because of dusk,
The long, forlorn, relentless trend
From larger day to huger night.

5

We wise, who with a thought besmirch
Blood over all our soul,
How should we see our task
But through his blunt and lashless eyes?
Alive, he is not vital overmuch;
Dying, not mortal overmuch;
Nor sad, nor proud,
Nor curious at all.
He cannot tell
Old men's placidity from his.

6

But cursed are dullards whom no cannon stuns,
That they should be as stones.
Wretched are they, and mean
With paucity that never was simplicity.
By choice they made themselves immune
To pity and whatever moans in man
Before the last sea and the hapless stars;
Whatever mourns when many leave these shores;
Whatever shares
The eternal reciprocity of tears.

Strange Meeting

It seemed that out of battle I escaped
Down some profound dull tunnel, long since scooped
Through granites which titanic wars had groined.

Yet also there encumbered sleepers groaned,
Too fast in thought or death to be bestirred.
Then, as I probed them, one sprang up, and stared
With piteous recognition in fixed eyes,
Lifting distressful hands, as if to bless.
And by his smile, I knew that sullen hall, –
By his dead smile I knew we stood in Hell.

With a thousand pains that vision's face was grained;
Yet no blood reached there from the upper ground,
And no guns thumped, or down the flues made moan.
'Strange friend,' I said, 'here is no cause to mourn.'
'None,' said that other, 'save the undone years,
The hopelessness. Whatever hope is yours,
Was my life also; I went hunting wild
After the wildest beauty in the world,
Which lies not calm in eyes, or braided hair,
But mocks the steady running of the hour,
And if it grieves, grieves richlier than here.
For by my glee might many men have laughed,
And of my weeping something had been left,

Which must die now. I mean the truth untold,
The pity of war, the pity war distilled.
Now men will go content with what we spoiled,
Or, discontent, boil bloody, and be spilled.
They will be swift with swiftness of the tigress.
None will break ranks, though nations trek from progress.
Courage was mine, and I had mystery,
Wisdom was mine, and I had mastery:
To miss the march of this retreating world
Into vain citadels that are not walled.
Then, when much blood had clogged their chariot-wheels,
I would go up and wash them from sweet wells,
Even with truths that lie too deep for taint.
I would have poured my spirit without stint
But not through wounds; not on the cess of war.
Foreheads of men have bled where no wounds were.

'I am the enemy you killed, my friend.
I knew you in this dark: for so you frowned
Yesterday through me as you jabbed and killed.
I parried; but my hands were loath and cold.
Let us sleep now ... .'

Exposure

Our brains ache, in the merciless iced east winds that knive us ...
Wearied we keep awake because the night is silent ...
Low, drooping flares confuse our memory of the salient ...
Worried by silence, sentries whisper, curious, nervous,
       But nothing happens.

Watching, we hear the mad gusts tugging on the wire,
Like twitching agonies of men among its brambles.
Northward, incessantly, the flickering gunnery rumbles,
Far off, like a dull rumour of some other war.
       What are we doing here?

The poignant misery of dawn begins to grow ...
We only know war lasts, rain soaks, and clouds sag stormy.
Dawn massing in the east her melancholy army
Attacks once more in ranks on shivering ranks of grey,
       But nothing happens.

Sudden successive flights of bullets streak the silence.
Less deathly than the air that shudders black with snow,
With sidelong flowing flakes that flock, pause, and renew;
We watch them wandering up and down the wind's nonchalance,
       But nothing happens.

Pale flakes with fingering stealth come feeling for our faces –
We cringe in holes, back on forgotten dreams, and stare,
    snow-dazed,
Deep into grassier ditches. So we drowse, sun-dozed,
Littered with blossoms trickling where the blackbird fusses,
            – Is it that we are dying?

Slowly our ghosts drag home: glimpsing the sunk fires, glozed
With crusted dark-red jewels; crickets jingle there;
For hours the innocent mice rejoice: the house is theirs;
Shutters and doors, all closed: on us the doors are closed, –
            We turn back to our dying.

Since we believe not otherwise can kind fires burn;
Nor ever suns smile true on child, or field, or fruit.
For God's invincible spring our love is made afraid;
Therefore, not loath, we lie out here; therefore were born,
            For love of God seems dying.

Tonight, this frost will fasten on this mud and us,
Shrivelling many hands, puckering foreheads crisp.
The burying-party, picks and shovels in shaking grasp,
Pause over half-known faces. All their eyes are ice,
            But nothing happens.

Futility

Move him into the sun –
Gently its touch awoke him once,
At home, whispering of fields half-sown.
Always it woke him, even in France,
Until this morning and this snow.
If anything might rouse him now
The kind old sun will know.

Think how it wakes the seeds –
Woke once the clays of a cold star.
Are limbs, so dear achieved, are sides
Full-nerved, still warm, too hard to stir?
Was it for this the clay grew tall?
– O what made fatuous sunbeams toil
To break earth's sleep at all?

CHAPTER 6

Owen's afterlife

Publication, critical reception, canonization

ON ARMISTICE DAY 1918 Harold Owen was serving with the Royal Navy off the coast of Victoria. Returning to his cabin, he found his elder brother sitting in a chair. Shocked, but not afraid, Harold asks of the soldier he knew to be serving on the Western Front, 'Wilfred, how did you get here?'

> He did not rise. … but his eyes which had never left mine were alive with the familiar look of trying to make me understand; when I spoke his whole face broke into his sweetest and most endearing dark smile. … He was in uniform and I remember thinking how out of place the khaki looked amongst the cabin furnishings. With this thought I must have turned my eyes away from him; when I looked back my cabin chair was empty … .
> Suddenly I felt terribly tired and moving to my bunk I lay down; instantly I went into a deep oblivious sleep. When I woke up I knew with absolute certainty that Wilfred was dead.[110]

The ghostly presence of his brother would haunt Harold for the rest of his life; his liberation from living in Wilfred's shadow would come only with the completion of Harold's three-volume family memoir *Journey from Obscurity*, published 1963–1965. That the brothers were only just getting to know each other as adults, beginning to leave behind their childhood and adolescent jealousies and frustrations, is one of the further ironies of Wilfred Owen's death in the last week of the war. In a letter to his brother, intended but never published as the introduction to *Journey from Obscurity*, and later privately printed as *My Dear Old Wolf* (1996) by John Bell, Harold noted that 'It is strange that I can still write to you and feel you are not dead at all.' Although Tom Owen 'went to France to visit the little churchyard in Ors' where his

Figure 53 Owen's permanent headstone at Ors. The quotation is taken from his poem, 'The End.' The certainty of the lines on the headstone is diametrically opposed to the message of the poem itself.

son was buried, Harold refused to do so: 'I dreaded the finality this would bring'[111] (figures 52, 53).

Owen the poet was virtually unknown in his own lifetime, except to a coterie of London literary figures and the readers of *The Bookman* and *The Nation*. Yet his reputation grew steadily, much to Susan Owen's delight, at the hands of editors who were also poets. Edith and Osbert Sitwell dedicated *Wheels 1919* to him, including seven of his poems in the anthology ('Strange Meeting', 'The Show', 'A Terre', 'The Sentry', 'Disabled', 'The Dead-Beat', 'The Chances') and, in 1920, *Poems by Wilfred Owen*, edited by Edith Sitwell and introduced by Siegfried Sassoon, was published by Chatto & Windus, with a second edition appearing the next year. By 1922, therefore, the *Manchester Guardian* reviewer of *Poems of To-day* (published by Sidgwick & Jackson) could remark specifically about the absence of Owen from the collection:

> How is it that a book that draws 'mostly from younger men who have written mainly under the influence and reactions of the war' has left out Wilfred Owen, who by that token should have been the very first choice?

Another poet and war veteran, Edmund Blunden, edited *The Poems of Wilfred Owen* in 1931, adding notes and a memoir. Although W.B. Yeats famously refused to include Owen in his edition of the *Oxford Book of Modern Verse* (1936) on the grounds that 'passive suffering is not a subject for poetry', the poets of the 1930s, including Dylan Thomas, Cecil Day Lewis, Stephen Spender, Louis MacNeice and W.H. Auden, 'accorded him the status of saint and martyr'[112] – representative of all the innocent young men cut down by politicians and generals. Recalling Owen's comment to his mother in 1918, that 'Fame is the recognition of one's peers', Dennis Welland noted, 'here, it would seem, was fame in abundance'.[113]

Owen's work, among that of his contemporaries, continued to influence the poets of later conflicts, particularly those of the Second World War. In

Figure 54 Susan Owen and her sister Emma Gunston, 1920.

Figure 55 *p.127* Manuscript page of 'The Send Off', 1918. The poem was drafted at Ripon in April–May 1918 and revised at Scarborough in July.

response to the question 'Where are the War Poets', the pre-eminent poet of 1939–1945, Keith Douglas, who was later killed at Normandy in 1944, voiced the anxiety of influence: 'hell cannot be let loose twice: it was let loose in the Great War and it is the same old hell now … . Almost all that a modern poet on active service is inspired to write, would be tautological.'[114]

Despite the passage of nearly a hundred years since his death, Owen continues to be a touchstone for commentators and poets reflecting on conflict in the twenty-first century. This has much to do with the essential humanity that permeates his work, fashioned from his own suffering and his pity for that of others, whether it be the poor in Dunsden or the soldiers of the Western Front. The power of his writing not only derives from this intense sympathy, but is a creative response to the texts, poets and writers he studied assiduously over the years. From the Bible and the English Romantics, to French Symbolists and modern poets including Yeats, Monro, Tagore and Sassoon, Owen mined works for his own interpretations of his lived experience as a young student, a vicar's lay assistant, a teacher and finally an army officer. Poems such as 'Anthem for Doomed Youth', 'Dulce et Decorum Est' and 'The Send-Off' (figure 55) respond to patriotic rhetoric and enlistment enthusiasm; 'Disabled' and 'Mental Cases' dramatize the living hell of physical and psychological wounds; while 'Miners' and 'Strange Meeting' (figure 57) are just two of the poems that mark Owen's obsession with the human body and its frequent descents underground. Despite being rooted in the cataclysm of 1914–18, they transcend their historical period.

Our image of Owen himself, his character and his personality, has been greatly shaped by his friends, including Osbert Sitwell and Sassoon. Radio broadcasts in the 1940s and 1950s kept his legacy alive for a wider audience, but his reputation grew exponentially in the 1960s, beginning with Dennis Welland's *Wilfred Owen: A Critical Study* (1960). Benjamin Britten incorporated Owen's poems in his *War Requiem* (1962), composed to consecrate the new Coventry Cathedral, one of the symbols of recovery from the destruction caused by Second World War bombing raids. In 1963 Cecil Day Lewis edited a new collection of Owen's poetry, including in it Blunden's earlier memoir

The ~~Draft~~. Send-off.

         close
own the ~~deep~~ darkening lanes they sang their way ~~to the siding she~~
o the siding-shed,
     ~~packed~~
nd ~~filled~~ the train with faces grimly gay.
    lined

heir breasts were stuck all white with wreath and spray
As men's are, dead.

Dull porters watched them, and a casual tramp
Stood staring hard,
Sorry to miss them from the upland camp.
   Then ~~signals~~, unmoved, signals
Unmoved, the ~~signal~~ nodded, and a lamp
Winked to the guard.

         ~~hushed up~~ wrongs hushed up
So secretly, like ~~men~~ ashamed, they went.
They were not ours:
We never heard to which front these were sent.

Nor there if they yet mock what women meant
Who gave them flowers.

Shall they return to beatings of great bells
In wild trainloads?
A few, a few, too few for drums and yells,
    creep ~~drag back~~ silent ~~strange silent~~
May ~~creep~~ back, ~~silent~~, to ~~still~~ village wells,
  hobble
Up half-known roads.

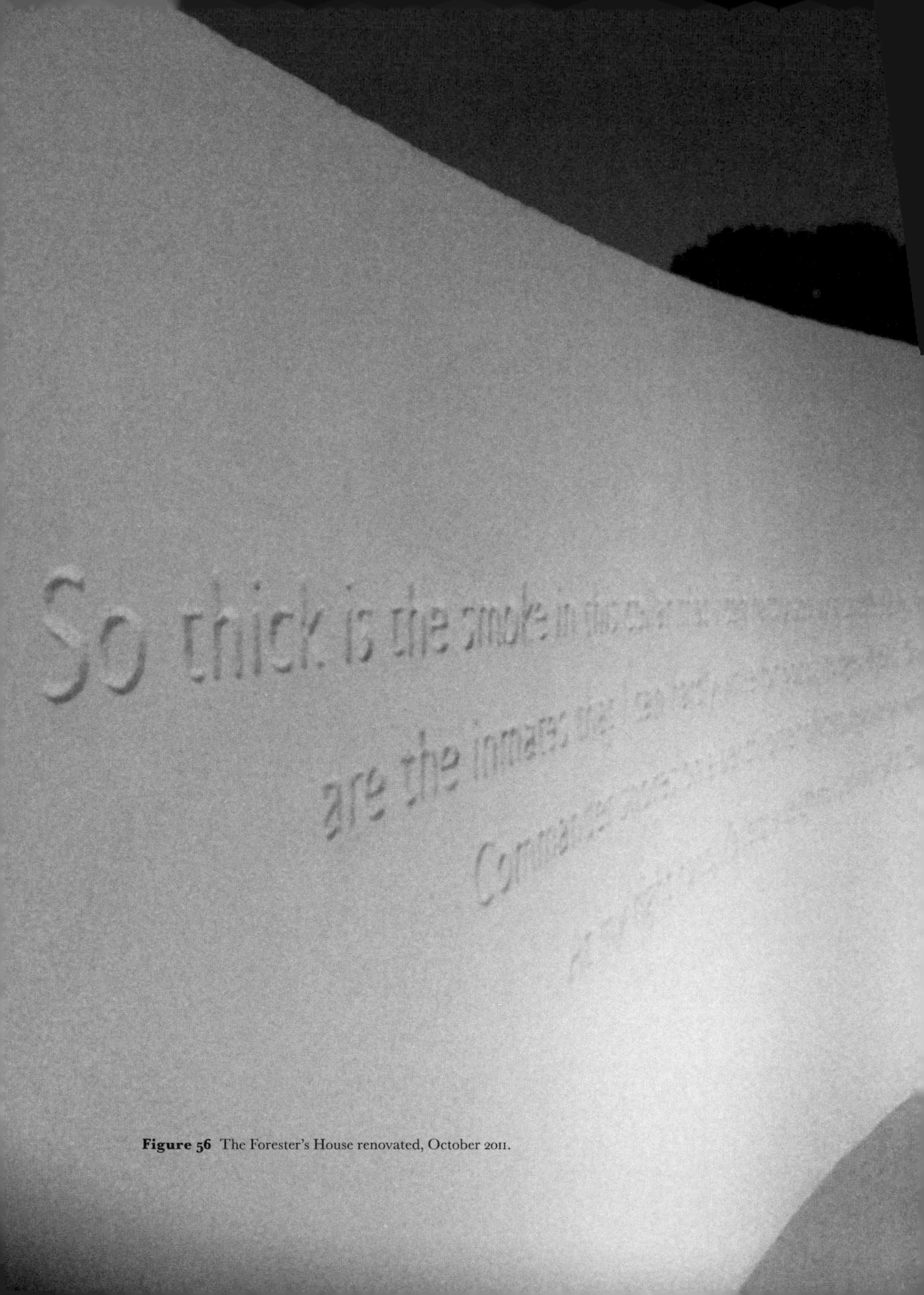

So thick is the smoke in those where the smoke of

are the inmates trap

Comman

Figure 56 The Forester's House renovated, October 2011.

and adding nineteen poems. Owen's work had particular resonance in that turbulent decade, seemingly complementing and reinforcing the critical re-evaluation of 1914–1918 in works such as Alan Clark's study *The Donkeys* (1961) and Joan Littlewood's Theatre Workshop production *Oh, What a Lovely War!* (1965).

In collaboration with John Bell, Harold Owen followed up *Journey from Obscurity* with the publication of the *Collected Letters* in 1967. (A smaller *Selected Letters* was edited by John Bell in 1985 and 1998.) Owen's official biography was written by yet another poet, Jon Stallworthy, and published to great acclaim in 1974 (new edition 2013). Stallworthy went on to edit *The Complete Poems and Fragments* (1983; new edition 2013) in two volumes, which brought all of Owen's work from his juvenilia to his mature poems together for the first time with the most accurate dating of the manuscripts to that time.

Sustained critical studies continued into the following decades, most notably by Dominic Hibberd, whose *War Poems and Others* (1973) and *Owen the Poet* (1986) set him on the path to becoming Owen's second biographer. *Wilfred Owen: A New Biography*, painstakingly researched and highly detailed in its appraisal of its subject, was published in 2002 and widely praised. Other scholars have explored aspects of Owen's life and work from varied perspectives, including Douglas Kerr in *Wilfred Owen's Voices: Language and Community* (1993), Santanu Das in *Touch and Intimacy in First World War Literature* (2005), and Guy Cuthbertson in *Wilfred Owen* (2014).

The issue that continues to interest, as well as vex, readers of Owen the most is his sexuality. Dominic Hibberd categorically states in his 2002 biography that Owen was 'gay' and suggests various liaisons, conjectured through his readings of the poems, letters and the reminiscences of others. There is, however, no historical evidence of any sexual encounter. While the male body and male relationships played a central role in Owen's emotional and literary life and while he might have shared Sassoon's homosexual orientation, 'given his strict evangelical upbringing and his indoctrination in the cult of "cleanliness", it is doubtful whether Owen would have "lain" with the anonymous "ghosts" in Canongate or Covent Garden'.[115]

As Santanu Das perceptively argued, an 'ambiguous zone' exists between 'diffuse homoeroticism and more common acts of homosexual intention', and 'a more nuanced understanding of gender and sexuality' will help us to appreciate more fully the 'intense homosocial world' that Owen describes with 'particular power'.[116]

Owen's international appeal may be seen through translations of his work, most notably by Joachim Utz (*Wilfred Owen: Gedichte*, 1993), Xavier Hanotte (*Et chaque lent crépuscule*, 2001) and Evgeny Lukin (*ПОЭМЫ*, 2012). Xavier Hanotte's play *La Nuit d'Ors: Fantaisie dramatique en trois tableaux* (2012) imagines Owen's final evening before the battle at the Sambre–Oise Canal.

The arts more broadly have embraced Owen's work. Playwrights, including Stephen MacDonald in *Not About Heroes* (1982), have explored his life and the lives of his contemporaries, while novelists such as Susan Hill in *Strange Meeting* (1971) found inspiration in his message and Pat Barker in her *Regeneration* trilogy (1991, 1993, 1995) featured him as a character in the first and third novels. Numerous television and radio documentaries over the years have added to Owen's popular appeal and recognition. It was in 1948 on the BBC Third Programme, presented by Laidman Browne, that Sassoon proclaimed 'Strange Meeting' Owen's 'ultimate testament, his passport to immortality and his elegy for the Unknown Warrior of all nations'. In additional to choral and classical composers, contemporary songwriters have embraced Owen's work, including the American alternative rock band 10,000 Maniacs on their album *Hope Chest* (1990).

Plaques and memorials in England and Scotland are numerous. His name joins those of his contemporaries on a memorial stone in Poets' Corner, Westminster Abbey, the words of his famous manifesto – 'My subject is War, and the pity of War. The Poetry is in the pity' – encircling them all. More modest plaques may be found at Plas Wilmot, now a listed building in Oswestry, the Owens' houses in Birkenhead (Elm Grove) and Shrewsbury (Monkmoor Road), and the Borage Lane cottage in Ripon where Owen wrote and revised his most famous poems in the spring of 1918. A plaque in the Regimental Chapel at Manchester Cathedral commemorates his service

Strange Meeting.

out of the battle
It seemed that ~~from~~ my ~~dugout~~ I escaped
Down some profounder tunnel, ~~older~~ scooped
                    long since
                    dull
Through granites which ~~the nether~~ flames had groined.
                     ~~pru~~ ~~titanic~~ wars

~~Down all its length~~
Yet also there / encumbered sleepers groaned,
Too fast in thought or death to be bestirred.
Then, as I probed them, one sprang up, and stared
With piteous recognition in fixed eyes,
Lifting ~~his~~ distressful hands, as if to bless.
And by his smile, I knew we stood in ~~hell~~.
~~As By his~~ ~~smile~~ I knew that sullen hall.—
                          pains
~~Yet slumber droned all down that sullen hall.~~
                            visions,
With a thousand ~~fears~~ that ~~creature's~~ face was
                                          grained;
              reached him there
Yet no blood ~~jumped here~~ from the upper ground,
         gun
And no ~~shell~~ thumped, or down the flues made moan.
But all was sleep. And no voice called ~~for men~~."
           friend," I said "Here is no cause to mourn."
"Strange~~My~~
"None", said that other. "Save the undone years,
The ~~hopelessness~~. Whatever hope is yours,
     ~~in achieved~~   ~~hunt for~~ ran wild
Was my life also; ~~comrade~~.
After the wildest beauty in the world,
Which lies not calm in eyes, or braided hair;

with the Manchester Regiment and his name may also be found in its Roll of Honour. There is a stained-glass window in Birkenhead Central Library, and in Oswestry there are a bench and plaque at St Oswald's Church and a Wilfred Owen Green. A major sculpture by Paul de Monchaux, *Symmetry*, sits in the grounds of Shrewsbury Abbey. Owen's time as a teacher is recognized by the Wilfred Owen School in Shrewsbury for children of primary and nursery age and a Wilfred Owen Building at Birkenhead Sixth Form College. Streets have been named after him: there are two Wilfred Owen Closes, one in Shrewsbury, one in Wimbledon (near Clement Avenue, where his cousins the Gunstons once lived) and a Wilfred Owen Way in Birkenhead. Craiglockhart, now a campus of Napier University in Edinburgh, boasts the War Poets Museum, and Owen's time in the city is also commemorated by a plaque at the Edinburgh Golf Club. All of these memorials testify to the many local people and groups who have claimed Owen as a famous son.

Out of one of these groups emerged the Wilfred Owen Association (WOA), founded in Shrewsbury in 1989 to promote Owen's life and work on a large scale. With Peter Owen, the poet's nephew, as president and hundreds of members in the UK and abroad, it organizes talks and meetings, publicises events by others on its website, and publishes a biannual Journal featuring contributions from academics, independent scholars, writers and poets. The WOA sponsors the Wilfred Owen Poetry Awards to recognize the achievement of poets whose work has an affinity with Owen's. Recipients include Seamus Heaney, Tony Harrison, Michael Longley, Jon Stallworthy and Gillian Clarke. The association also supports new and emerging poets at the Tŷ Newydd National Writers' Centre of Wales with a Wilfred Owen bursary.

It is perhaps most poignant that Owen has memorials, too, in France, including a plaque at the Marie at Joncourt and at the lock at the Sambre–Oise Canal. The Infant School at Ors inaugurated the Wilfred Owen Médiathèque in 2008. Most significantly, every year on 4 November the tiny village commemorates the British poet with a procession to and a ceremony at his grave, which lies in the Communal Cemetery, where he is buried alongside Second-Lieutenant Kirk, posthumously awarded the VC, and twenty-two other ranks were who were killed that day in 1918. L'Association Wilfred Owen France, in conjunction with the tireless efforts of the mayor of Ors, Jacky Duminy, secured funding to save and redevelop the Forester's House (Maison forestière de l'Ermitage) outside the village, where Owen wrote his last letter. Designed by the British artist Simon Patterson, the brick building has been transformed into a permanent memorial and was opened to the public in October 2011 (figure 56).

Inevitably, in this digital age Owen has a large presence on the Internet. Numerous websites, including the First World War Poetry Digital Archive, showcase and offer resources for the study of his work, including digitized images of the manuscripts, while Facebook and Twitter have helped to engage readers and enthusiasts of all ages in discussion. YouTube features numerous readings of Owen's poems by, among others, Dylan Thomas, Kenneth Branagh, Sean Bean, Christopher Hitchens and Ben Wishaw – alongside clips of Samuel West, Stuart Bunce and others portraying Owen on screen.

The physical objects themselves have their own interesting history. Owen's manuscripts, letters and other personal items were in the care of Susan Owen until her death in 1942, when they passed to Harold. They are now cared for by various institutions. Sassoon launched an appeal for the British Museum to acquire the main poetry manuscripts for the nation, which he presented in two bound red volumes in 1934. Owen's letters were sold to the University of Texas at Austin in 1970, where they form part of the Wilfred Owen War Poetry Collection at the Harry Ransom Humanities Research Center. Owen's personal library, schoolbooks and family photographs were bequeathed to the English Faculty Library at Oxford by Harold's widow Phyllis in 1975. In this latter sense, Harold's words ring poignantly true: 'So you see, Old Wolf, although you could not get to your coveted Oxford, your work has done this for you'[117] (figure 58).

Thus while Owen acknowledged in his 1918 Preface that his elegies 'are to this generation in no sense consolatory', his hope that they may be to the next continues to be fulfilled.

Figure 57 *p.131* Manuscript page of 'Strange Meeting', 1918. The manuscripts suggest that Owen may not have regarded 'Strange Meeting' as complete. It was drafted between January and March 1918 probably at Scarborough but possibly at Ripon.

Figure 58 *below* Framed locket with Owen's portrait, now at the English Faculty Library, University of Oxford.

Disabled

He sat in a wheeled chair, waiting for dark,
And shivered in his ghastly suit of grey,
Legless, sewn short at elbow. Through the park
Voices of boys rang saddening like a hymn,
Voices of play and pleasure after day,
Till gathering sleep had mothered them from him.

* * *

About this time Town used to swing so gay
When glow-lamps budded in the light blue trees,
And girls glanced lovelier as the air grew dim, –
In the old times, before he threw away his knees.
Now he will never feel again how slim
Girls' waists are, or how warm their subtle hands.
All of them touch him like some queer disease.

* * *

There was an artist silly for his face,
For it was younger than his youth, last year.
Now, he is old; his back will never brace;
He's lost his colour very far from here,
Poured it down shell-holes till the veins ran dry,
And half his lifetime lapsed in the hot race
And leap of purple spurted from his thigh.

* * *

One time he liked a blood-smear down his leg,
After the matches, carried shoulder-high.
It was after football, when he'd drunk a peg,

He thought he'd better join. – He wonders why.
Someone had said he'd look a god in kilts,
That's why; and maybe, too, to please his Meg,
Aye, that was it, to please the giddy jilts
He asked to join. He didn't have to beg;
Smiling they wrote his lie: aged nineteen years.
Germans he scarcely thought of; all their guilt,
And Austria's, did not move him. And no fears
Of Fear came yet. He thought of jewelled hilts
For daggers in plaid socks; of smart salutes;
And care of arms; and leave; and pay arrears;
Esprit de corps; and hints for young recruits.
And soon, he was drafted out with drums and cheers.

* * *

Some cheered him home, but not as crowds cheer Goal.
Only a solemn man who brought him fruits
Thanked him; and then enquired about his soul.

* * *

Now, he will spend a few sick years in institutes,
And do what things the rules consider wise,
And take whatever pity they may dole.
Tonight he noticed how the women's eyes
Passed from him to the strong men that were whole.
How cold and late it is! Why don't they come
And put him into bed? Why don't they come?

Mental Cases

Who are these? Why sit they here in twilight?
Wherefore rock they, purgatorial shadows,
Drooping tongues from jaws that slob their relish,
Baring teeth that leer like skulls' teeth wicked?
Stroke on stroke of pain, – but what slow panic,
Gouged these chasms round their fretted sockets?
Ever from their hair and through their hands' palms
Misery swelters. Surely we have perished
Sleeping, and walk hell; but who these hellish?

– These are men whose minds the Dead have ravished.
Memory fingers in their hair of murders,
Multitudinous murders they once witnessed.
Wading sloughs of flesh these helpless wander,
Treading blood from lungs that had loved laughter.
Always they must see these things and hear them,
Batter of guns and shatter of flying muscles,
Carnage incomparable, and human squander
Rucked too thick for these men's extrication.

Therefore still their eyeballs shrink tormented
Back into their brains, because on their sense
Sunlight seems a blood-smear; night comes blood-black;
Dawn breaks open like a wound that bleeds afresh.
– Thus their heads wear this hilarious, hideous,
Awful falseness of set-smiling corpses.
– Thus their hands are plucking at each other;
Picking at the rope-knouts of their scourging;
Snatching after us who smote them, brother,
Pawing us who dealt them war and madness.

The End

After the blast of lightning from the east,
  The flourish of loud clouds, the Chariot Throne;
After the drums of time have rolled and ceased,
  And by the bronze west long retreat is blown,
Shall Life renew these bodies? Of a truth,
  All death will he annul, all tears assuage?
Or fill these void veins full again with youth,
  And wash, with an immortal water, age?

When I do ask white Age, he saith not so:
  'My head hangs weighed with snow.'
And when I hearken to the Earth, she saith:
  'My fiery heart shrinks, aching. It is death.
Mine ancient scars shall not be glorified,
Nor my titanic tears, the seas, be dried.'

NOTES

1   Wilfred Owen, Selected Letters, ed. John Bell, Oxford University Press, ed. 1998, p. 359.

2   Harold Owen, Journey from Obscurity, vol. I, Oxford University Press, 1963, p. 7.

3   H. Owen, Journey from Obscurity, vol. I, p. 19.

4   H. Owen, Journey from Obscurity, vol. I, pp. 150–151.

5   H. Owen, Journey from Obscurity, vol. I, p. 151.

6   H. Owen, Journey from Obscurity, vol. I, p. 85.

7   H. Owen, Journey from Obscurity, vol. I, p. 103.

8   Dominic Hibberd, Wilfred Owen: A New Biography, Phoenix, 2003, p. 37.

9   H. Owen, Journey from Obscurity, vol. I, p. 176.

10   Jon Stallworthy, Wilfred Owen, Oxford University Press, 1974, p. 48.

11   W. Owen, Selected Letters, pp. 10–11.

12   H. Owen, Journey from Obscurity, vol. II, p. 217.

13   W. Owen, Selected Letters, p. 16.

14   W. Owen, Selected Letters, p. 16.

15   W. Owen, Selected Letters, p. 16.

16   W. Owen, Selected Letters, pp. 158–159.

17   H. Owen, Journey from Obscurity, vol. I, pp. 251–252.

18   W. Owen, Selected Letters, pp. 28–29.

19   W. Owen, Selected Letters, p. 31.

20   W. Owen, Selected Letters, p. 43.

21   W. Owen, Selected Letters, p. 53.

22   W. Owen, Selected Letters, p. 66.

23   W. Owen, Selected Letters, p. 32.

24   W. Owen, Selected Letters, p. 50.

25   Jon Stallworthy, 'Owen, Wilfred Edward Salter (1893–1918)', Oxford Dictionary of National Biography, Oxford University Press, 2004 [www.oxforddnb.com/view/article/37828, accessed 27 Nov 2013].

26   W. Owen, Selected Letters, p. 67.

27   Hibberd, Wilfred Owen: A New Biography, p. 120.

28   W. Owen, Selected Letters, p. 68.

29   Stallworthy, 'Owen, Wilfred Edward Salter (1893–1918)', Oxford Dictionary of National Biography.

30   W. Owen, Selected Letters, p. 90.

31   W. Owen, Selected Letters, p. 88.

32   W. Owen, Selected Letters, p. 88.

33   W. Owen, Selected Letters, p. 89.

34   W. Owen, Selected Letters, p. 142.

35   W. Owen, Selected Letters, p. 146.

36   W. Owen, Selected Letters, p. 89.

37   W. Owen, Selected Letters, p. 92.

38   W. Owen, Selected Letters, p. 108.

39   W. Owen, Selected Letters, p. 116.

40   W. Owen, Selected Letters, pp. 108–109.

41   W. Owen, Selected Letters, p. 114.

42   W. Owen, Selected Letters, p. 109.

43   W. Owen, Selected Letters, p. 110.

44   Hibberd, Wilfred Owen: A New Biography, p. 165.

45   W. Owen, Selected Letters, pp. 118–119.

46   W. Owen, Selected Letters, p. 119.

47   W. Owen, Selected Letters, p. 122.

48   W. Owen, Selected Letters, p. 130.

49   W. Owen, Selected Letters, p. 153.

50   W. Owen, Selected Letters, p. 132.

51   W. Owen, Selected Letters, p. 168.

52   W. Owen, Selected Letters, p. 169.

53   W. Owen, Selected Letters, p. 168.

54   W. Owen, Selected Letters, p. 171.

55   W. Owen, Selected Letters, p. 172.

56   W. Owen, Selected Letters, p. 173.

57   Stallworthy, Wilfred Owen, p. 29.

58   W. Owen, Selected Letters, p. 173.

59   Wilfred Owen: Collected Letters, eds Harold Owen and John Bell, Oxford University Press, 1967, p. 367.

60   W. Owen, Collected Letters, p. 369.

61   W. Owen, Collected Letters, p. 369.

62   W. Owen, Selected Letters, p. 179.

63   Stallworthy, Wilfred Owen, p. 134.

64   W. Owen, Selected Letters, pp. 181.

65   W. Owen, Selected Letters, p. 182.

66   W. Owen, Selected Letters, pp. 181–182.

67   W. Owen, Selected Letters, p. 184.

68   Hibberd, p. 239.

69   H. Owen, Journey from Obscurity, vol. III, 1965, pp. 152–153.

70   W. Owen, Selected Letters, p. 203.

71   W. Owen, Selected Letters, p. 203.

72   W. Owen, Selected Letters, p. 207.

73   W. Owen, Selected Letters, pp. 208–209.

74   W. Owen, Selected Letters, p. 210.

75   W. Owen, Selected Letters, p. 210.

76   W. Owen, Selected Letters, p. 212.

77   W. Owen, Selected Letters, pp. 213–214.

78   W. Owen, Selected Letters, p. 214.

79   W. Owen, Selected Letters, pp. 214–215.

80   W. Owen, Selected Letters, p. 215.

81   W. Owen, Selected Letters, p. 215.

82   W. Owen, Selected Letters, p. 227.

83   W. Owen, Selected Letters, p. 238.

84   W. Owen, Selected Letters, p. 238.

85   W. Owen, Selected Letters, p. 239.

86   W. Owen, Selected Letters, pp. 243–244.

87   W. Owen, Selected Letters, pp. 246–247.

88   Stallworthy, Wilfred Owen, p. 192.

89   Stallworthy, 'Owen, Wilfred Edward Salter (1893–1918)', Oxford Dictionary of National Biography.

90   W. Owen, Selected Letters, p. 280.

91   W. Owen, Selected Letters, pp. 265–266.

92   W. Owen, Selected Letters, pp. 269–270.

93   W. Owen, Selected Letters, p. 271.

94   Stallworthy, 'Owen, Wilfred Edward Salter (1893–1918)', Oxford Dictionary of National Biography.

95   D. Hibberd, Owen the Poet, Macmillan, 1986, p. 99.

96   W. Owen, Selected Letters, p. 289.

97   W. Owen, Selected Letters, p. 296.

98   W. Owen, Selected Letters, pp. 305–306.

99   W. Owen, Selected Letters, p. 321.

100   W. Owen, Selected Letters, p. 328.

101   W. Owen, Selected Letters, p. 328.

102   W. Owen, Selected Letters, p. 311.

103   W. Owen, Selected Letters, p. 329.

104   Three Poets of the First World War: Ivor Gurney, Isaac Rosenberg and Wilfred Owen, eds J. Stallworthy and J. Potter, p. 110.

105   Hibberd, Wilfred Owen: A New Biography, p. 411.

106   W. Owen, Selected Letters, p. 351.

107   W. Owen, Selected Letters, p. 352.

108   W. Owen, Selected Letters, p. 362.

109   W. Owen, Selected Letters, p. 362.

110   H. Owen, Journey from Obscurity, vol. III, pp. 198–199.

111   Harold Owen, My Dear Old Wolf, The Backwater Press, 1996, p. 6.

112   Stallworthy, 'Owen, Wilfred Edward Salter (1893–1918)', Oxford Dictionary of National Biography.

113   Dennis Welland, Wilfred Owen: A Critical Study, Chatto & Windus, rev. ed. 1978, p. 138.

114   Keith Douglas, 'Poets in this War', in The Letters, ed. Desmond Graham, Carcanet, 2000, p. 352.

115   Santanu Das, Touch and Intimacy in First World War Literature, Cambridge University Press, 2005, p. 140.

116   Das, Touch and Intimacy in First World War Literature, p. 26.

117   H. Owen, My Dear Old Wolf, p. 8.

BIBLIOGRAPHY

Editions

The Complete Poems and Fragments of Wilfred Owen, 2 vols, ed. Jon Stallworthy, Oxford University Press, Oxford, 1984; new edition, Chatto & Windus, London, 2013.

The Poems of Wilfred Owen, ed. Jon Stallworthy, Chatto & Windus, London, 1990.

Selected Letters of Wilfred Owen (new edition), ed. Jane Potter, Oxford University Press, Oxford, 2015.

Wilfred Owen: Collected Letters, eds Harold Owen and John Bell, Oxford University Press, Oxford, 1967.

Wilfred Owen: Selected Letters, ed. John Bell, Oxford University Press, Oxford, 1998.

Wilfred Owen: War Poems and Others, ed. Dominic Hibberd, Chatto and Windus, London, 1973.

Translations

Hanotte, X., *Et chaque lent crépuscule*, Le Castor Astral, Bordeaux Cedex, 2001.

Lukin, E., *ПОЭМЫ*, St Petersburg, 2012.

Utz, J., *Wilfred Owen: Gedichte*, Mattes Verlag, Heidelberg, 1993.

Biography

Cuthbertson, G., *Wilfred Owen*, New Haven and London, Yale University Press, 2014.

Hibberd, D., *Wilfred Owen: A New Biography*, Phoenix, London, 2002, pb 2003.

McPhail, H., *Wilfred Owen: Poet and Soldier*, Gliddon Books / The Wilfred Owen Association, Norwich, 1993.

Owen, H., *Journey from Obscurity: Memoirs of the Owen Family*, 3 vols, Oxford University Press, Oxford, 1963–1965.

Owen, H., *My Dear Old Wolf: An Undelivered Letter to Wilfred Owen from his Brother Harold*, The Backwater Press, Wooton-by-Woodstock, Oxfordshire, 1996.

Stallworthy, J., *Wilfred Owen*, Oxford University Press, Oxford, 1974, rev. ed. Pimlico, London, 2013

Criticism

Bäckman, S. *Tradition Transformed: Studies in the Poetry of Wilfred Owen*, C.W.K. Gleerup, Lund, 1979.

Bergonzi, B. *Heroes' Twilight: A Study of the Literature of the Great War*, Constable, London, 1965; new ed., Carcanet, Manchester, 1996.

Das, S., *Touch and Intimacy in First World War Literature*, Cambridge University Press, Cambridge, 2005.

Douglas, K., *The Letters*, ed. Desmond Graham, Carcanet, 2000.

Hibberd, D., *Owen the Poet*, Macmillan, Basingstoke, 1986.

Kendall, T. (ed.), *The Oxford Handbook of British and Irish War Poetry*, Oxford University Press, Oxford, 2009.

Kerr, D., *Wilfred Owen's Voices: Language and Community*, Oxford University Press, Oxford, 1993.

Stallworthy, J., *Survivors' Songs: From Maldon to the Somme*, Cambridge University Press, Cambridge, 2008.

Welland, D., *Wilfred Owen: A Critical Study*, rev. ed., Chatto & Windus, London, 1978.

Williams, M., *Wilfred Owen*, Seren, Bridgend, 1993.

First World War Poetry Anthologies

A Corner of a Foreign Field: The Illustrated Poetry of the First Word War with Photographs from the Daily Mail, Atlantic Publishing, London, 2007.

Giddings, R., *The War Poets: The Lives and Writings of the 1914–1918 War Poets*, Bloomsbury, London, 2000.

Stallworthy, J., *Anthem for Doomed Youth*, Constable & Robinson, London, 2002.

Stallworthy, J. and Potter, J. (eds), *Three Poets of the First World War: Ivor Gurney, Isaac Rosenberg and Wilfred Owen*, Penguin, London, 2011.

LIST OF POEMS

PICTURE CREDITS

The following images are from the Wilfred Owen Archive at the English Faculty Library, University of Oxford, reproduced with kind permission of the Trustees of the Wilfred Owen Estate: p. 2, f.cc(b); p. 7, f.cc(a); fig. 2, Box 36, 2A a; fig. 3, Box 36, 2A d; fig. 4, Box 36, 1A a; fig. 5, Box 32, item 22; fig. 6, Box 36, 2A c; fig. 7, Box 36 1A e; fig. 8; fig. 9, Box 36, 1A b; fig. 10, Box 36, 1A d; fig. 11, Box 36 1A g; fig. 12, Box 36, 2b a; fig. 13, Box 36, 2B b; fig. 14a, Box 28, Book 4; fig. 14 b and c, Box 28, Book 4; fig. 15, Box 36, 2B c; fig. 16, Box 34, 4A d; fig. 17, Box 36, 1B a; fig. 18, Box 34, 4B a; fig. 19, Box 36 1C a; fig. 20, Box 36 1C b; fig. 21, Box 36, 2C b; fig. 22, Box 35, 8I/J I; fig. 23, Box 36, 2D a; fig. 24, Box 34, 4B b; fig. 25, Box 36, 2D e; fig. 26, Box 34, 4B b; fig. 27, Box 36, 5BLc; fig. 28, Box 36, 2D c; fig. 29, Box 34, 4A e; fig. 30, f.cc483r; fig. 31, f.2e; fig. 32, f.1d(a); fig. 35, Box 36, 5BL a; fig. 36; fig 39, Box 34, 4C a; fig. 41; fig. 42; fig. 43a, Box 34, 4A b; fig. 43b, Box 34, 3I/J e; fig. 44, f.2e(c)l; fig. 45, f.cc529; fig. 46, f.cc528; fig. 47, f.lfl; fig. 49, Box 35, 8L d; fig. 50, Box 28; fig. 51, Box 28; fig. 52, Box 28; fig. 53, Box 28; fig. 54, Box 35, 8L c; fig. 56, f.cc487r; fig. 60, Box 32, item 23.

The following images are © British Library Board / The Wilfred Owen Literary Estate: fig. 1, Add. MS. 43720, fol. 1; fig. 37, Add. MS. 43720, fol. 21; fig. 57, Add. MS. 43720, fol. 18; fig. 49, Add. MS. 43720, fol. 3.

The following images are reproduced by courtesy of the University Librarian and Director, The John Rylands Library, The University of Manchester. By kind permission of the Wilfred Owen Estate: fig. 33, DSW/1/1/4/5/4; fig. 34, DSW/1/1/4/5/2.

The following images are © The First World War Poetry Digital Archive / Kate Lindsay: fig. 38; fig. 55. Fig. 40 © National Portrait Gallery, London; fig. 48 © The Harry Ransom Center / The Wilfred Owen Literary Estate; fig. 58 © Jane Potter.

INDEX